Love at the Pub

Love at the Pub

*An Insider's Guide to Craftsmanship, Conversation,
and Community at the Brick Store Pub*

Mary Jane Mahan

iUniverse, Inc.
New York   Bloomington

iUniverse books may be ordered through booksellers or by contacting:

iUniverse
1663 Liberty Drive
Bloomington, IN 47403
www.iuniverse.com
1-800-Authors (1-800-288-4677)

Because of the dynamic nature of the Internet, any Web addresses or links contained in this book may have changed since publication and may no longer be valid. The views expressed in this work are solely those of the author and do not necessarily reflect the views of the publisher, and the publisher hereby disclaims any responsibility for them.

ISBN: 978-1-4401-7035-5 (sc)
ISBN: 978-1-4401-7036-2 (ebook)

Printed in the United States of America

iUniverse rev. date: 10/06/2009

To Mug and Pug,
better known as Mom and Dad,
the best parents any child could wish for

Thank you for giving abundantly from your heart and
demonstrating the richness of what counts,
the currency of love

Contents

Preface

Michael Gallagher

It was January 1997 and high time to find the money to open the Brick Store Pub. My two business partners and I had a business plan, a vision, and a love for great beer. The problem was that we only had a baseball card collection and three "junker" cars for collateral. This obviously was going to be a challenge, however we were determined.

We were as nervous as schoolboys before we cleaned ourselves up to go visit Jimmy Dickey at Sun Trust Bank. "Oh for the love of Pete, I guess we have to put on suits," I said. "I mean, that's what you do when you go to get a loan, right?" *Great.* "Is it brown shoes and belt or black shoes and belt with a blue suit?" one of my partners asked, and then decided, "Ah the heck with it." We took a quick shot of Irish whiskey and trotted down to see the man behind the desk.

At the time, everyone in Decatur knew us as bartenders and baristas. So our impression on our banking neighbor was amusing at best. "Yeah, that's great Jimmy. We appreciate you laughing at our choice of dress," we silently told him as we walked out of the financial institution empty handed. "And yes, of course we understand why you can't give us the money. We'll get it somehow. We just gotta."

Three months and seven banks later, we finally secured a modest loan from SouthTrust Bank. So began our adventure of opening a neighborhood pub.

It seemed pretty simple: find a great location, hire good people, train them well, and treat them right. We knew what we didn't want: no TVs, no neon signs, and no light beer. We had a few solid ideas of what we did want—to pour only world-class beer, offer an out-of-the-park whiskey selection, and serve honest food at great prices. We also wanted to be a positive force in the community with involvement on every level and, of course, play fantastic music (but not too loud). First and foremost, we wanted to be surrounded by good people.

Although opening the Pub wasn't quite as easy as we imagined, it came together pretty well with a lot of hard work, help, and great, good people. Mary Jane Mahan was one such soul. If anyone is able to take an accurate snapshot of where we started and compared it to how we've grown as a community-minded pub, it's Mary Jane. She has worked and volunteered with us right from our start, participated in our staff celebrations and pub parties, and witnessed our progression. She's been at the Brick Store Pub to see friends, stop by for a quick bite to eat, and even get a ride home from the airport. Hot date? You betchya. You name it, Mary Jane's been there.

Lots of places say they are a "family restaurant." But the real question we should ask them is: What does family mean to you?

Your family knows who you really are. As much as Mary Jane, or MJ as we like to call her, has watched us grow, we have done the same for her. As she's told us many times (and it's true), we are her southern family through thick and thin. In reading this book, I had a feeling of seeing a familiar childhood friend who knows entirely too much about you and your past (in a good way). I'm glad to say MJ knows the Brick Store like that.

Very few people have been a part of our work, personal, and community lives on a weekly and daily basis since the Brick Store's beginning. It was a real treat to be able to read about our history and philosophy from a family staff member. I even learned a thing or two about the people and the place myself. I know you'll enjoy it as well.

Foreword

Paean to a Perfect Pub
Ray Oldenburg

In 1946, George Orwell published a fictional account of his dream pub, "The Moon Under Water." He stipulated ten key points for a perfect drinking haven that included a quiet atmosphere, friendly barmaids who know you by name, cheap and solid food, proper drinking vessels, draught stout, a snack bar, and a garden. Since then, many real pubs have adopted the name of Orwell's ideal pub and many others have sought to realize Orwell's vision to the letter. But should that fictional pub be considered the ultimate goal for any publican seeking to provide the best for his customers? Is it possible to create a pub that *exceeds* Orwell's vision?

I believe such a pub exists in Decatur, Georgia. The Brick Store Pub opened in 1997 with a determination to do everything right and then improve on it. Mary Jane Mahan's account of its evolution is a great pleasure to read and the depth of her research is an education in all aspects of running a pub. If, for example, you think you know beer, you're in for an awakening. There is a plethora of beer styles and varieties that many have never dreamed existed. One can safely predict that our nation's bottle shops will feel the impact from an educated populace determined for imbibing adventure.

The Brick Store Pub lacks Orwell's snack bar or his garden, but it has taken on goals unimagined by the author. The owners and the staff have worked to cultivate customers' tastes—gently leading them away from mass-produced beer, such as Coors, to a higher standard of Warsteiner, and ultimately on to independent American beers, such as Victory Prima Pils. They succeed Orwell's vision in the food menu as well, creating beer dinners with dishes to complement the various kinds of beer served.

The Brick Store Pub was created at an opportune time when the nation's microbreweries were beginning a strong ascent. Americans were discovering a taste for beer beyond basic levels of consumption and spreading its gospel. The owners of the Brick Store Pub constantly stayed ahead of this trend—every factor contributing to the ultimate enjoyment of the convivial pint was taken into account and implemented.

The beer movement was similar to the concurrent "third wave" of coffee in the mid-2000s. This theory described the first wave of coffee as proliferation of coffee for its existence as a hot, pleasing, caffeinated drink. The second wave saw an elevation of coffee quality and an explosion of espresso beverages across the world. According to barista professional and Murky Coffee proprietor Nicholas Cho, the third wave is "letting the coffee speak for itself."

In 2004, Georgia abandoned the six percent alcohol limit on beer, thus opening the door to gourmet bars. The Brick Store Pub created its jewel, an 800 square-foot Belgian Bar exquisitely done in Trappist styling. This addition hailed and cemented the Brick Store Pub as one of the finest in the country.

Much of the charm and appeal of the Brick Store Pub can be found in what it has chosen to not offer. There are no "lite" beers, pitchers, beer specials, neon signs, or daily television. It is a place where people drink, talk, and behave well in an atmosphere ideally suited to promoting conversation and enjoyment of life. The author has achieved a classic that will encourage significant improvements in the nation's beverage industry.

The Brick Store Pub should be applauded because it almost immediately became an exemplary "third place," a place apart from home and work where community is formed; where people from different walks of life get to know one another, meet regularly, and talk. Talk is the real music of a pub and in its context democracy thrives.

Acknowledgments

It took an entire village to nurture this book into existence. I salute Dave Blanchard, Michael Gallagher, and Tom Moore for their bravery in opening the Brick Store Pub. Thank you for giving me a job and for generously supporting this project.

Thank you to all the City of Decatur pioneers and the Brick Store Pub community. Huge thanks to every person who contributed a story, bought me a beer, and gave encouragement.

A million thanks to all staff of the Brick Store Pub (past and present). You answered my bottomless questions, pointed me in the right direction, shared your insights, and put up with my book tab. A special *grazie* to Dayna Cotter, Rachel Adams, Ben Karp, Eric Ottensmeyer, Laura Hull, Matt Christison, Bill McJenkin, Shannon Barnes, Kelley Turner, and Carol Blanchard.

Many times I felt at an utter loss of what to do next. Someone always appeared to lend me a hand. So I extend my warm gratitude to Volkmar Wochatz, Nick Purdy, Dan Adamson, Lyn Menne, Linda Harris, Lee Ann Harvey, Helen Wallington, Lance Haugan, Daren Wang, Alison Valk, and Joanne Chu.

I know very little about the technicalities of beer. I just drink it. Many craft beer industry folks lent me their expertise. I give a special little bow to Bob Townsend, Jessica Moss, Rob Nelson, Dennis Lange, Lee Dickson, Miles Macquarrie, Meredith, and Simon.

To my coach Amy Scott Grant and my editor Stephanie Gunning, thank you each for your brilliant skills, laughter, and unwavering support—what great investments!

Love to Ted, Sherri, Leefa, Chrisy, and my family. Without you, why bother?

"Beer is proof that God loves us and wants us to be happy."
—Benjamin Franklin

Introduction

There's a Little Beer Pub in Decatur . . .

Imagine this. Based on numerous recommendations you decide to venture into the shopping district of a small community that sits right on the borderline of a large southern United States metropolis. For eons all you've heard are rave reviews of this family-friendly, quirky, laid-back town where the boutiques are yummy, schools are outstanding, socio-demographics hit every color of the rainbow, and the beer, well, you've heard endlessly about this little beer pub.

Welcome to Decatur, Georgia, where Mayberry meets Berkeley, six miles due east of downtown Atlanta. An award-winning city, Decatur stands out as a pedestrian-friendly "smart growth poster child," with 200 storefronts, restaurants, galleries, services, and entertainment venues that offer you an experience decidedly "mallternative." Decatur is also home to the Brick Store Pub, a cultural phenomenon and entrepreneurial anomaly where you feel as if you are in your favorite brother's living room every time you walk in the door. It's a place where people are likely to know your child's name as well as that of your dog, even offering Fido a drink (of water).

Perhaps a friend or coworker told you about it. Maybe a family member marched you through the door. If you live in metro Atlanta undoubtedly you've been hearing about "this beer pub in Decatur" for months (if not years) passionately described as the "Mecca" of great beer and conversation. One thing is for certain: a single trip to this magical, delightful place and you will fall in love with it. From then on you will go there with (or without) your friends and family on every possible occasion.

The Brick Store Pub (also known as the Brick Store or simply the Pub) teems with life and character. Weddings and wakes have been performed there. Baby showers, business meetings, and blowout parties occur on a regular basis. Celebrations of seasons and holidays are par for the course. The beer selection cycles more often than the full moon. The authentic fish and chips impress even the most seasoned travelers—that is, if they can locate the front door, as the Pub is wonderfully well hidden.

The parking is impossible. The window blinds are half closed. The wooden sign hanging off the façade is weather-faded and barely readable. You have to want to find this place, be determined even, as it is nestled off a cul-de-sac on the old downtown Decatur square (aka the Square). The only thing that makes it noticeable to pedestrians as a pub are a small chalkboard with quotations about drinking from notables, such as Benjamin Franklin and W.C. Fields, and three outside whiskey barrel tables adorned with German beer umbrellas. Well, that and the throngs of people young and old, who show up nightly to sip on pints and patiently wait for a table like wedding guests outside an old brick castle.

Now, although a goodly amount of beer does flow from the Brick Store and it is a charming building, there is no castle moat to cross or turrets to scale. In fact, get out of your head any notion of the Pub as an Irish-themed imposter (think fake telephone booths) or a beer-tourist attraction, as the locals are upset enough that they have to jockey for a table on a Wednesday night. The only thing decidedly Irish about the Pub is its lyricism and love of people. As an unknown author once captured, "the Irish don't care what you do, they care who you are."

"Everybody has to believe in something…I believe I'll have another drink."

—W. C. Fields

So why do they flock here? And why is it described at the heartbeat of Decatur? Perhaps it's the delightful notion of relaxing and drinking really good beer with great friends. There's also a refreshing diversity of age, class, color, occupation, and sexual orientation found scattered through the establishment. The fact that there are no TVs or loud music is a godsend. The certainty of fast, delicious, reasonably priced food (along with properly served beverages) is thankfully assured. You always score big with the visiting parents or in-laws who unanimously approve of your home away from home. After all, Guinness is good for children (just kidding). You run into neighbors that you actually want to see. The preserved character of the old building offers a bona fide pub feel that does not insult your sensibility. To seal the deal—you're welcomed by professional and personable staff who obviously are treated like "real people" by their employers. Now that's priceless.

Thank you, Brick Store Pub.

Why We're Here

There are many good pubs out there, but only a few really reach an extraordinary level of quality like the Brick Store Pub. National recognition includes *Forbes Traveler* (top 10 bar list, 2008), Esquire. com (second top bar, January 2009 rankings), and CNN (Atlanta destinations, 2008). In the beer world, the Brick Store receives high praise from the two biggest and most respected online beer review websites. In 2008 *BeerAdvocate* rated it America's #2 Best Beer Bar on Planet Earth and Ratebeer.com gave it the distinction of World Class Beer Bar. Local accolades hail year after year from critic and reader reviews in *Creative Loafing's* Best of Atlanta.

What this book, *Love at the Pub*, aims to convey is the greatness of the Brick Store Pub and its evolution from neighborhood revitalization anchor business to renowned beer destination. Yet this tale is something far beyond the resounding cheers for world class beer. This is the decade-plus celebration story of the Pub, the owners who built it, and the essence of the community who gathers there. As patron Melissa Grace shares, "Once you get the perfect beer, maybe the perfect appetizer, and you are surrounded by friends, there is no better feeling on earth."

A powerful overall love of this establishment was revealed in the data collected from over 120 interviews, 100 online surveys, as well as hundreds of existing Internet patron reviews. The same themes emerged:

> We love the Pub for its authenticity, warmth, and charm. We love its generosity, spirit, and dedication. We love the beer, the staff, the atmosphere, and the

owners. We love it because we feel relaxed the moment we walk in the door. We love that it is a pub and not a bar where our children are welcome, where we see our neighbors, where we are never embarrassed about bringing someone here as our guest. We love Decatur and we love how the Pub meshes perfectly with our community. "I met my wife there." "We had the big conversation of starting a family in a window booth." "We are planning a Brick Store love child."

Brick Store Pub at Christmas time

What You Won't Find in Here

What you hold in your hands is an unabashed ode to the Brick Store Pub evidenced by well over two hundred folks who shared their "Brick Story." Such an account deserves a brief mention of the obvious, namely that this establishment is run and staffed by human beings who all have their up and down days. For ordinary reasons, there are those who don't love the Pub (just one single sour grape online survey submission). There have been periods as well where staff energy was off-kilter and communication was not flowing (sounds like most marriages, yes?). What's remarkable, however, is the overall dedication and rock solid consistency that unifies the Pub. In its twelve-year history, less than ten people have been fired and only one employee has ever walked out during a shift (that's a great exception in this industry). Instead of airing dirty laundry or illustrating love at the Pub through what it is *not*, this tale accentuates the positive and keeps the focus where it deserves—on examples that inspire us all to our own personal and professional greatness.

Several beer suppliers and distributors who contributed to this book acknowledge that while the Brick Store is a mighty big national player, it is far from the only one. And thank goodness, as the Pub owners are as eager as anyone to see the continued growth of the craft beer movement. "Imitation is the sincerest flattery," says English sportsman Charles Caleb Colton. So while this book touts the excellence of the Pub, know that it is in great company. For instance, upon learning that the Brick Store is ranked as America's number two beer bar on BeerAdvocate.com, folks always ask, "What's number one?" That answer is Ebenezer's Pub in Lovell, Maine. If you visit, be sure to tell them Decatur says "hello."

Another thing barely discussed in this yarn is the beer cellar that the guys are creating in an old bank vault underneath the Square. Stay tuned for more on this très cool, potential-laden space as for now the vault is considered the "man hut" for Lee Dickson, Brick Store manager (and Pittsburgh beer geek who practically sat on the Pub steps until he was hired.) For that matter, the rich history of the British "public house" started in the 1800s is not discussed either. In its place is the importance of Ray Oldenburg's "third place" theory. As this book went to print, I met a wonderful woman from County Claire, Ireland, who gave testimony to the darker potential of Pub culture when drinking becomes the centerpiece of community life. May this serve as a good reminder to all of us, and thankfully this is not the case of Decatur or the Pub.

Javamonkey is another big piece of local history that is not covered in here. This wonderful independent coffee house is the former Church

Street Coffee, the first "Decatur Caffeinator" at the top of the city's renaissance. Dave, Mike, and Tom bought that business in October 1999, renovated it, renamed it Javamonkey, and then sold it in April 2006 to two "family members" (a former Brick Store employee and a Decatur High School alum). Located out the Pub's back door, down through the alleyway, and directly across the street, Javamonkey is considered a favorite cousin among Brick Store staff and management.

In a nut shell, Javamonkey is no longer direct lineage because the guys discovered their true passion—superb beverages and fun, casual dining (coffee shops being a very different animal). This is precisely why they decided to open another restaurant right around the corner in Decatur, a bouncing baby boy named Leon born in February 2009. Leon's Full Service, a community-driven restaurant and bar, is now delighting folks with specialty cocktails, delicious craft beer, an expansive menu with a Belgian flair, and a bocce court. As Leon's is still spanking wet behind the ears, his story is still developing and will have to wait. Love at the Pub is the matriarch's tale, so let's get back to her.

125 East Court Square circa 1865

Why Is It Called the Brick Store?

As the Brick Store honeymoon continues through this day, we're all still very proud, and patiently correct all who butcher the name. "Where is the Brick House? Um, the Brick Stone? Brick Cellar? The Brick?" The correct name is *Brick Store Pub* located at 125 East Court Square, called so because it stands on the site of the old Ramspeck Building, a general store where they used to sell, among other things, bricks. Back then many locals called it the "brick store."

As the history goes, the general store burned down in 1890 and the lot was sold to Dr. Washington J. Houston Jr., a Decatur native and former government land surveyor on assignment in the Appalachian Mountains in northern Georgia. Tired of being away from his family, Dr. Houston switched to the medical profession and built his family home on the East Court Square lot in 1905. He ran his medical practice from the residence until 1929 when he decided to increase his income by having a brick commercial building constructed on the spot where his house stood. Jacking his house up from the foundation, Dr. Houston turned the house around and moved it to the rear of his property facing Church Street. The address was and still is today 418 Church Street.

The first occupant of the new commercial building known as 124–125 E. Court Square was a grocery store followed by L.D. Adams & Sons, a popular men and women's apparel store that stayed open well into the 1950s. In 1987, Dr. Houston's daughters sold their ownership in the Decatur city property to its present owner and Brick Store landlord, Mr. Glen Gurevich. Glen rented the 125 address to various businesses and opened his own place in the adjacent property, Sweet Melissa's (named for his daughter), a breakfast and lunch eatery, which continues to be a favorite Decatur staple.

A Rip-roaring Start

The doors of the Brick Store Pub proudly opened on Friday, June 27, 1997, at nine o'clock in the evening. Owners Dave Blanchard, Michael Gallagher, and Tom Moore had barely hammered in the last of the nails when they ran home for a fast shower and came back to sell their first official beer. They were welcomed with open arms as people were hungry and thirsty for a friendly pub atmosphere, and it soon evolved into an unofficial community center. Although the clientele built gradually, the Brick Store's growth was certain and strong. As one native describes it, "I've never seen a place open more smoothly or quickly." After watching restaurant after restaurant open and fail, the Pub's instant popularity created a sense of joy and pride among the Decatur residents.

Granted, none of this happened in a vacuum. It was an overnight success twenty years in the making thanks to many committed pioneers (see the Decatur story in Part Three). However, the charm of three fresh-faced young men with no business experience was an undeniable attractor factor. Here they were opening an audacious bar like no one had ever seen in the area—no light beer (no *domestic* beer, for Guinness' sake), no TVs, no beer specials, no pitchers, and no gimmicks. Plus they were welcoming children and grandparents along with the college crowd. On the surface, they were launching their concept in a location that on the surface appeared to be an economic dead zone. It was risky to say the least.

Yet, from very start of the Pub's build-out, it felt like someone had lit a powder keg. The years following the Brick Store's explosion marked a return to the Square's commercial health and a vim and vigor that had not been felt in many decades.

How on Earth They Did It (and Still Do)

The strength of a three-legged stool is undeniable. Thus it's fair to say that the Brick Store took off like a rocket because there were three invested owners on the premises. Not only did they divvy up the workload, they actually enjoyed working as a trio. The blending of their individual personalities created a bond of brotherhood that Dave, Mike, and Tom were able to leverage well.

For instance, the Brick Store boys enjoyed an immediate luxury of getting to know their patrons at length through owner "face-time". Their essence and vision was delivered straight from the source. Longtime regular Steve Bradshaw remembers: "On my first visit, Mike Gallagher was behind the bar, very sociable, and eager to share his knowledge. Because of the guys' unity and friendship, they inspired a camaraderie that made us want to bring all our friends here. It was really fun."

As observed by many regulars and most staff, the Pub "just works" because of the unique gifts and talents of each owner. In general, Dave leads on building the Brick Store's world of beer which encompasses the areas of industry relationships, product presentation, storage and maintenance issues, and cutting-edge trends. He also weighs in strongly on "front of house" operations, which is restaurant lingo for the working environment of a server and bartender. Mike functions as a natural statesman and leads on hospitality, special events, staff education, and hiring. He's also the Pub's de facto community grand master. Tom anchors the ship with his dedication to numbers crunching, book balancing, and "back of house" operations, which means everything in the kitchen. His food organizational chart would rival that of a military chow hall. All three men are in charge of drinking Jamison Irish Whiskey with the staff (a very important business clause) and getting to know as many neighbors as possible.

Brick Store Owners Tom Moore, Dave Blanchard, and Mike Gallagher

Grab a Seat (Brick Store Layout)

There are a thousand things to notice the second you enter through the wooden door of Pub. To the immediate left is a cozy square window nook that serves as a perfect hideout. This beer drinking fort is pressed against an oval booth enclosed with a stain glass window divider and wooden lamp post sentry. Continuing along the large, high northern wall are three booths that are bordered by a merchandise display case (you can pick up free beer magazines here). This flows into a fifteen-step wooden staircase that leads to the snug second floor seating area.

Up here you can plop yourself into the wall-length bench or take a bird's eye seat at two high balcony rail tables with tops handcrafted from wine boxes. You could also turn to the left and under the brick triple archway leading to the intimate second floor Belgian Bar.

Back downstairs and on the right, there is a large exposed brick wall with five old windows that open to an old alleyway. The front booth is a spacious window nook that flows into a long wall-length bench with four tables. A small sea of tables rest in the restaurant's center just behind the greeting stand (made from an old radio). This area is flanked by three high whiskey barrel tables that are an exact match to the trio of outdoor tables. Attractive and well maintained window planters, both inside and out, impart the earthy nature of the Pub.

Perhaps the most notable item inside the Brick Store is the back-centered, horseshoe-shaped bar that welcomes you to sit a spell on one of its twentyish barstools. This space is crowned by a large wooden chandelier and off-set by red model bi-plane whose five-foot wing span hangs precariously as if it were about to dive bomb the bar. On permanent loan from patron Bruce Wynn, the model was built in the 1950s by his father who flew radio-controlled planes most of his life. Other interesting collectables sit atop the high back bar structure accompanied by two large hanging chalkboards on the right that announce new and standard drink selections.

A Quick Pint: Roots and Inspiration

The roots of the horseshoe bar and general Brick Store concept came from a fine drinking institution in Athens, Georgia, named The Globe. Located on a prime corner in the heart of downtown, The Globe went against the grain of all other bars with its European feel, relaxed atmosphere, quiet music, and a complete lack of neon lights, TVs, or big-named brewery décor. It even served organic beer, a growing market today and ahead of itself in the early '90s. As a result, the focus remained on conversation and sampling of superior selection of beer, wine, single malt whiskey and scotch, and fine bourbon.

The naturally well-lit and cozy nooks of The Globe drew in refined palates like a magnet to come sit on their comfy sofas, rocking chairs, and wooden benches. Professors, graduate students, and well-cultured locals appreciated the daily offerings of world papers and complimentary bread and cheese in the late-afternoon. Sipping the likes of Moretti LaRossa and gazing at the large mural of fine beverage production felt like an escape from the mundane and ordinary. Here was a place for mature conversation. Here was a place that boasted distinction and beckoned drinking adventure. Here was a place that raised the bar on bars. Slip into the doors and enter a refreshingly different world.

It's certain that The Globe influenced many a lost college youth to take up the path of beer connoisseurship, including the Brick Store proprietors who spent plenty of time there in the early 1990s. Dave, Mike, and Tom all attended the University of Georgia and met each other while working in the same Mellow Mushroom pizza parlor. As the three Athens pals forged ahead with their dream, their inspiration for the Pub drew heavily on The Globe's concept, most notably the shiny, horseshoe-shaped bar, relaxed ambiance, and superior beer selection that went on to become the Brick Store's hallmarks.

The Young Waitress from Philadelphia

My story intersects with that of Dave Blanchard and Michael Gallagher in October 1994 in the aforementioned Athens Mellow Mushroom. I was a mess: twenty-two and fresh out of Villanova University, far away from my family, completely unprepared for graduate school, homesick, carless, and flat broke. My student loan was M.I.A., and I went down to my last $500 while living off baked potatoes and salsa. I stubbornly refused to call my parents for help. I felt trapped in my gigantic apartment dwelling with incompatible roommates. Topping the list, I had fallen into an instant, confusing relationship with my breezeway neighbor, a darling native Atlantan who made me venison steaks from his hunting trips (I soon became a vegetarian). The only thing I had going for me was that the Speech Communication graduate building lay just a stone's throw from the inviting business district. I escaped there often.

After a long day of pounding the pavements of downtown Athens looking for a waitressing job, I dragged myself into a stool at the 'Shroom. In an exhausted tone, I asked the bartender for some water, or "wooder" as it came out in my tired Philly accent. "Wooder? You must be from up North," asked the nice looking young man with piercing blue eyes, a black mane of hair, and a demeanor that reminded me of the Notre Dame Fighting Irish mascot. It was none other than Mike Gallagher.

Mike took pity on one of his own: an Irish Catholic, Philadelphia track runner. As I sat there and babbled my life story, Mike listened patiently and with a funny laugh asked me the obvious question: did I want to apply for a job? "Oh, uh, yeah I guess so," I muttered. His friendly ear had melted the stress just like that, even if only momentarily. Mike put an application and a pen in my hand and streamlined it to the owner. I got hired that week in the middle of the University of Georgia fall game season. I had no clue what I had just stepped into as I only knew Rocky Balboa as cultural religion, not southern college football.

The chance encounter with Mike in the 'Shroom not only changed my life, it saved my life. That dinky little restaurant job gave me critical friends, financial independence (including buying my first car), sanity and strength to finish grad school, and stability that otherwise would have seen me turn tail and run back home. I had more fun with our little band of pals than I have at any other time period of my life. Chalk it up to youth and freedom, however there was pure magic in those relationships and all the close times we had shutting down the bar, bonding over brunch, going to music shows, and playing three A.M. Frisbee golf. It was all about laughter and hard work done well. Oh, and drinking good beer until the wee hours at Booth One (or "one-ing it" in staff vernacular).

Dave was the ultimate pal. He not only scheduled me for big money shifts, he also found me a closer, safer, ultra cool place to live in Normaltown just a mile from work and school. Davey bailed me out of some very stupid life moments and brought me beer to Terrell Hall the night before I defended my thesis (not so good a choice). He's even in the video I used to interview student volunteers for my thesis project.

Mike, well, he kept me stocked in bear hugs. He was my touchstone and a bridge from my past to my present and future. I was a lost puppy and Mike played a crucial big brother role for me which I will be eternally grateful. We have been roommates, Music Midtown adventurers, workhorses, confidants, and Tuesday night pals. He's also been my boss.

See, I know intimately how Dave, Mike, and Tom treat their employees and how much the Pub meant to Decatur because I had the privileged good fortune to be on the opening year staff (tenth hired on the payroll). The week I was to make a major move in Athens, I changed my mind and picked up the phone to call Dave. "Can I have a job?" Of course, he replied. "Come now." Come I did four days later just as the Pub opened their doors. And again, that decision changed and saved my life. I took root in Decatur in 1997 and enfolded into this darling town that has served as my southern home ever since.

I felt very humbled to serve as "the pen" for our community chronicle, tasked with capturing a love that needed no words. I interviewed and surveyed every person possible including the butcher, the baker, and the candlestick maker. What poured forth was a passion for the Brick Store that left me speechless at times. Before this, I had seldom reflected on its special nature as it was an unspoken truth imprinted in my bones. I was like a spoiled kid who didn't know how good she had it in her own family until someone nudged me to speak up and write (by the way, that "someone" was the Pub itself).

As the stories passionately poured in, I finally let myself feel the immense scope of this project. It sunk in that the subject of my first book was not only regarding my adulthood home and extended family but also on a cornerstone of the community and our common bond. It felt intimidating at times, however the support I received was tremendous, much like when I trained around Decatur for my first (and only) charity marathon in 1998. Almost every night I worked at the Pub during the four month period, many customers would say they saw me running. I'd hear cheers of "Go, MJ!" as I ran down Ponce de Leon. The Pub even let me hold a fundraiser.

It took me five-and-a-half hours to complete that 26.2 mile run and it took me over five years to finish this book marathon (again receiving encouraging smiles and cheers of "Go, MJ!"). I felt a strong desire for it to mirror the greatness of our city and our Pub with its anchoring presence in so many lives. The most astonishing of all was the gift I received back as writing this story allowed me to re-experiencing and expand my own love of the Pub in beautiful, soulful new ways.

Capturing the *Love at the Pub* narrative was the most professional fun I've ever experienced. Not only have I loved beer since age eight (starting with baby sips of my dad's Schlitz), the Brick Store makes for an amazing subject. Who wouldn't want the Belgian Bar as their dream office? As I did fact checking via the whiskey chalk board amid the 2009 St. Patrick's Day party, I was tickled to be reminded that I've volunteered for the Great Decatur Beer Festival since its inception. That investment has given me the esteemed title of *beer captain*, a moniker close to my heart as a token sign of my place in the community. I do declare, however, after writing all these Brick Stories that my new favorite role is *seanchai*, Gaelic for Irish storyteller.

A Solid Trinity: Organization of Love at the Pub

The essence of my love for the Pub mirrors that of many other staff members: stability, kindness, and fun. However, this is not a single employee account of working at the Pub. Not even close. This book reflects the collective voice of everyone who comes into contact with the Brick Store.

About one hundred online survey submissions yielded a plethora of information, as did more than 120 interviews that took place over two years. A blurb in the *Decatur Dispatch* resulted in several phone calls from residents of turn-of-the-century families who shared priceless history and photos. Dave and Mike opened their rolodexes, while the bartenders put me in touch with many essential regulars. Spontaneous conversations frequently occurred in the bar, and over time I was handed off like a relay race baton, "Oh, you should talk to this person…"

The danger of meeting community members at the Pub, however, is that there is always great beer involved. While Charles Bukowski and Ernest Hemmingway can hold down a drink and a pen, I was useless after even a light session around the horseshoe bar. Thankfully, the project picked up pace once I banned myself from the Brick Store and switched to phone interviews.

From these data, I gleaned three major themes that serve as pillars of love at the Brick Store Pub: craftsmanship, conversation, and community.

The first pillar is craftsmanship. This pillar builds a bridge from the brewery to the barstool, reporting from a variety of professionals who drink in the folklore of world-class beer and call the Brick Store "the place where everybody in the beer industry goes." Hear from independent artisan brewers, beer distributors and suppliers, importers and exporters, servers and bartenders, regulars, and, of course, the visionary owners of the Brick Store Pub. From special events to everyday drinking, craft beer is held in a most deserving light that shines through the best presentation, promotion, and caretaking possible. Learn about beer styles courtesy of adapted definitions from BeerAdvocate.com.

Craftsmanship at a glance looks like the whimsy of ordering a cider and having it arrive in a teacup instead of a glass (100 percent proper for a Dupont Cidre Bouche). On paper, it is the "365 Days" report from one of the Brick Store's main distributors that they have gone through a keg of Weihenstephaner every day for the last year. In brick and mortar, it's the famed Belgian Bar, the second-story addition that made it possible to become a top-tier beer establishment. On the palate, it's the monthly beer and cheese pairing, and the beer dinners, and the semi-monthly tap handle rotation. In a word, craftsmanship at the Pub is "dynamic."

The second pillar is conversation. At the Brick Store Pub, conversation is king. The buzz of lively human exchange fills the bar with an electric feeling of authentic connection. Consider the importance of conversation and places like the Pub via the "third place" theory of sociologist Ray Oldenburg, Ph.D. Whereas first place is home and second place is work, the third place is where we go to connect informally and publicly with our community. Third places like the Brick Store are what bind us together as society and make life a richer experience. Pull up a stool and learn how the owners gave the neighborhood something to talk about as they built their dream bar from the ground up with sweat equity. Follow their journey from the time they met to the moment got their business lease to the night they sold their first official beer. Catch a glimpse of what makes their partnership work. Finally, listen to a few staff members share their memories of how the Pub got built and the role it has played in their lives.

The third pillar is community. While the greatness of the Pub stems from leadership, its richness lies in community ties. Here you'll begin to understand why Decatur is considered a sensational small town. Think like a local as city stakeholders and residents pour into the Pub and pour out their hearts about this family-friendly environment with strong young adult appeal. As one patron effused, "I can't wait to see the next ten years." A short visit to some of Decatur's festivals paints the picture of how community events are interwoven with the fabric of Brick Store living, in particular the Great Decatur Beer Festival. Be a fly on the wall for some of the romances and marriages that took root and were celebrated inside those hallowed brick walls. Finally, take an inside peek at some of the employee "holidays" as they clearly illuminate the wisdom that charity begins at home.

Let's Get to the Beer

I really hope you are reading this book while at the Pub with a great beer, wine, or sweet tea in your hand. Absolutely make sure you come to visit (the South is wonderful). For that is the only way to truly experience what all the locals and beer lovers and community members know by way of the heart via that creaky wooden door…that our community is rare and important that and our the Pub is a living, breathing vessel of fellowship, kindness, excellence, and mysticism. And absolutely good, plain, silly fun, too! It is one of the most singular working experiences available in the restaurant industry and the joy of Decatur, as you are about to read from many people. We deserve many more Brick Store Pubs in the world for every reason imaginable.

Enjoy, and I'll see you at the Pub.

Part One

Craftsmanship

"A beer never has been and never will be served in a 16-ounce shaker pint glass at the Brick Store Pub."

—Dave Blanchard, Brick Store Pub co-owner and beer bar visionary

As all the locals know, a trip to the Brick Store Pub is like entering a Hobbit's portal into a wonderland where pretension does not exist, stress evaporates, and service goes the extra mile. The main event for many, however, is the art-in-a-glass beverages that drop down on your table like European magic. We come here to drink the best beers in the world—beer we love with a passion. Why?

Why Beer Anyway?

Maybe it's in our blood. Consider that beer brewing is as ancient as the hills. Not only is beer known as the mother of all beverages (with due respect to its own mother: water), beer manufacturing tops the list of the world's oldest industries. Beer even has an ancient drinking song, "The Hymn to Ninkasi" (for the Mesopotamian goddess of brewing) which calls us to imbibe beer in a "blissful mood." According to a 2,000 B.C. provisions list found on an Assyrian tablet, beer would have been carried on Noah's ark. In short, beer has brought people together since the dawn of civilization, "and way before then," quips local beer expert Jessica Moss.

Beer is significant in all cultures and on every continent, serving as a beloved companion on life's highway. It's a mark of celebration for the new Decatur mother, who after birthing plans to send her husband to the Brick Store for take-out food and to-go Belgian ale (or so she fantasizes). It's sacred tradition in Tibet, where the groom's uncle shares three toasts of beer with the bridesmaids pre-wedding eve. It's a familiar comfort to the Irish family in Philadelphia, who after the death of their father hold a seven-day wake with family and friends, drinking beer and whiskey in a non-stop flow.

"Beer is what you drink as you sit around to figure out *it*, whatever *it* is," insists owner Dave Blanchard. "That's why I love it." Apparently beer is nothing short of your soul's trusted medium. If you're going to figure out your life, do it with the best beer available. You might be able to write your own version of *War and Peace* as good beer they have a-plenty at the Brick Store Pub. The all-star international drink menu boasts seventeen tap handles and a 70-bottle cooler served through the main bar and eight Belgian tap handles and 125-bottle cooler served through the upstairs Belgian Bar. Not a lame pick in the lot, oh blessed be her holy name De Dolle Brouwers Dulle Teve 10° (Mad Bitch).

In a world of overwhelming mediocrity, the manner in which the Pub delivers gourmet beer is elevated to mastery. It's a privilege to drink here. You wouldn't park a Ferrari in a pigsty, and you certainly wouldn't serve Orval Trappist ale in a Solo plastic cup (think keg stand parties). The Pub's status as a top ten American beer bar is an outstanding accomplishment that reflects a reverence for craftsmanship on all levels.

Belgian Pale Ale (Orval): Initially brewed to compete with pilsners during World War Two. Less bitter than other regional pale ale, aged hops are used to create a delicate hop finish. It boasts sweetish to toasted malt overtones. They should be decanted properly, leaving the yeast in the bottle, as this will showcase their brilliant color range from pale straw yellow to amber hues. Most Belgian pales are crowned with thick, clinging, rocky white heads.

Local Darling to Rising National Star: An Evolution

The Brick Store website says it all: "Drink good beer." While this remains a simple philosophy, in the late 90s it was delicate to wean an entire neighborhood off its familiar draught selections while maintaining excellent customer relations. Not only did the owners do so with grace and style, they also took the high road of respect regarding the transition from Bud to Belgian, Bass to Lagunitas, Red Stripe to Oskar Blues, Peroni to Victory, Stella to St. Bernardus, Newcastle to Brooklyn, domestic to Dogfish, uninteresting to Unibroue. Wee-wee-wee all the way home to Sweetwater and Terrapin, our Georgia independent staples.

"Um, yes, I'll have another Schneider Aventinus," orders the stay-at-home mom with authority, kids and hubby in tow. Belly up Brick Store-style. To this day, "Can I order a Bud Light?" is never met by Pub staff with arrogance or haughtiness, rather it's embraced with enthusiasm. After all, here's another homerun opportunity to turn someone away from the world of mass-produced, mass-marketed, watered-down beer and give that person an exciting alternative. The Pub owners love a challenge. (*Tip:* Most successful people love challenges).

The Brick Store opened June 1997 with great anticipation from the Decatur community who at first probably wanted nothing more than a really good, solid, friendly place to eat and drink beer. *What* exactly they'd be drinking perhaps never crossed their minds. We've only got a handful of choices, right? Wrong. Way wrong.

A whopping 97 percent of total U.S. breweries (1,483 out of 1,527) are small, independent, traditional craft breweries according to the Brewers Association 2008 industry report. In fact, craft brewers have seen their sales soar by 58 percent since 2004. "The strength of this correlates with the American trend of buying local products and a preference for more flavorful foods and beers," said Paul Gatza, Director of the Brewers Association.

Then why does Unibroue La Fin Du Monde not immediately roll off everyone's tongue as "tripel liquid gold" whereas many of us can recall a NFL Superbowl beer commercial with little effort? Easy, it's the power of marketing. Yet, if you pay attention, you will see the undeniable evidence of craft beer's influence on the mega-breweries (such as advertising campaigns that boast "freshly brewed with special hops"). So even though Big Beer Industry's foothold in the American consumer consciousness is considerable, it's not set in stone. There are a growing number of ale drinkers just waiting to be tapped for the great exploration of fine beer consumption.

Tripel (La Fin Du Monde): Brewers use up to three times the amount of malt to make a tripel than to make a standard Trappist "simple." A triple is traditionally bright yellow to gold in color with aroma and flavor running along complex, spicy, powdery yeast, and fruity with a sweet finish. Its sweetness comes from both pale malts and higher alcohol content. Its head should be big, dense, and creamy. Its light body is produced from the use of Belgian candy sugar (up to 25 percent sucrose), which adds notoriously strong alcohol aromas and flavors. Yet, the best-crafted ones hide this character quite deceivingly, making them sipping beers.

An Authentic Reputation: Built and Earned

Sure, the Brick Store carries the best and some of the hardest-to-find beers in the world. That is far from the only reason it receives top ratings and reviews from the likes of *Forbes* and *BeerAdvocate*. The Pub blossomed from neighborhood bar to national rising star based on a number of factors. Stocking the cooler with a plethora of gourmet beverages was just one of them. Another distinction of the Brick Store is its symbiotic relationship with everyone who comes in contact with it, including brewers, distributors, staff members, guests, and community groups. It goes right down to the mailman and keg delivery driver (both of whom prefer the Brick Store for their weekend pint sessions, by the way).

People across the country know the Brick Store Pub, especially in the industry. The guys' love, respect, and enthusiasm for the international beer community radiates like a beacon. In fact, it's frequently the case where the Pub's lively interest in a certain beer will outpace that of its distributor. A brewery might even do a special release just for the Brick Store.

A shining example of mutually supportive partnerships starts with, of all things, a shiny beer can. Here's a story that starts in Lyons, Colorado, at the home of the Oskar Blues Cajun Grill and Brewery, aka "The Little Brewery that Cans."

Oskar Blues Ten FIDY Russian Imperial Stout, rated "Beer of the

Year" by *The Denver Post*, is a giant in its category yet looked rather dwarfish when it came out on the market packaged in four-and-a-half inch aluminum cans. Because distributors are used to seeing independent craft beer displayed in beautiful, tall bottles, Ten FIDY in a can conjured images of high school keg parties not high standards. Didn't we try to impress our teenaged friends by crushing cheap cans of Schlitz and Genesee Cream Ale against our foreheads? (Little did everyone know that fresh craft gourmet beer in cans was soon to become the market rage, and that the Oskar Blues boys had stumbled upon this by accident. But shhhh, that's a whole 'nuther story.)

Russian Imperial Stout (Ten FIDY): Inspired by brewers in the 1800s to win the heart of the Russian czar, this is the king of stouts, boasting high alcohol by volume and plenty of malt character. It has low to moderate levels of carbonation and huge, roasted chocolate and malt flavors. Often dry, it has suggestions of dark fruit. Flavors of high alcohols are quite evident. Hop character can vary from none to balanced to aggressive.

Fast forward to the desk of Henry Monsees, owner of Savannah Distributing Company near Georgia's Atlantic coast, who did a double take when he first laid eyes on the Ten FIDY beer can in his catalogue circa 2006. Ten FIDY as a trendsetter was completely lost on the southern gent, as he asked with incredulity, "What on God's green earth is that?" Henry ordered a sample can just to see what it looked like on his file cabinet. When it arrived, Henry was befuddled: "Ten who? Someone named a beer this?"

At a total loss, Henry tossed the can to one of his Atlanta sales reps and said to Simon, "Take it to those Brick Store boys. They'll try just about anything." Davey and Mikey instantly became infatuated with this decadent 10 percent alcohol by volume (ABV) chocolate milkshake and pushed Henry to get them the first kegs available out of Colorado. Ten FIDY soon rocked the Brick Store main bar, as staff, patrons, and the general beer community clamored for pints of this heavenly malted milk ball dream.

The Decatur-Ten FIDY love affair grew into near obsession. The next winter season, Dave asked for every keg that came into Georgia and he got them. Other bars grumbled, however the facts stood for themselves. That Colorado imperial stout flowed out of the Brick Store just as fast as it washed in. Oskar Blues sales manager Wayne Anderson was willing to take some gripes to please an establishment that had been a loyal fan of his beer since day one. "We credit the Brick Store with much of our success," says Wayne. "Not only do they embody the best of what this industry's about, they are simply the coolest, most down-home, salt-of-the-earth guys. We feel like we are home every time we're there."

Meanwhile, back in Mr. Monsees' Savannah Distribution office, Henry weighed the pros and cons of approving Dave's Ten FIDY keg request. He knew others might be miffed, however Henry recalled when Savannah got into the game of craft beer in 2004. Like others, his company took advantage of a change in state laws that essentially opened the Georgia market for gourmet high gravity beer. Back then, Savannah had about twenty beers total in their portfolio. Today, they have 780. Henry credits the Brick Store for showing *his* company the demand for high quality beer and championing Savannah's foray into the risky business of premium, pasteurized, perishable keg products. "We could not have done what we've done without them," Henry says of the Pub owners.

As Georgia's oldest beer distributor (after Prohibition) stepped up to carry the world's most selective beers, such as Oskar Blues, Henry got a phone call one day from Dave thanking Savannah Distribution for their commitment. The University of Georgia grad was blown away and thought, "Aren't I supposed to be calling and thanking *you*?" Those types of account phone calls are few and far between in Henry's field and a pleasure to receive. But what else would you expect from those "unusual guys" at the Brick Store who are always on the edge of what's new?

To put this conversation into perspective, most beer kegs cost somewhere between seventy to one hundred dollars each. The barrels at the Brick Store cost in the neighborhood of $250. To this day some of Henry's friends in the business tell him he's crazy. Mr. Monsees himself had to be convinced that a customer would be willing to lay down seven to twelve dollars for a beer. He stopped scratching his head once the Brick Store invoices started piling up. As Henry puts it, "When you're taking twenty to forty kegs to one little old account in Decatur, you sit up and take notice."

The Bottom Line: Passion

Two things about Dave Blanchard are clear: his keg lines and his bottom line. "It's never about the money," the visionary asserts. "Once you focus on money alone, you're screwed." This operating philosophy of the guys is key to the Brick Store's distinctive evolution, and it mirrors that of Dave's close colleague, mentor, and specialty beer supplier Darius Debski of D&V International. Mr. Debski says of his own business decisions, "Belgian beers are the best in the world, made by masters. Why would I care about anything else?" The specialist knows other merchandiser might make bigger profits from trends or dealing in cheaper products, however this gourmet sees no point in simplistic thinking. "There's no passion in asking, 'What's my bottom line?' There's nothing wrong with that. I just don't find it personally rewarding."

This is exactly why Darius admires and appreciates working with Dave Blanchard, a man as far away from the nickel-and-dime attitude as you could possibly get. Darius recalls the Brick Store's extravagant request for St. Bernardus Abt. 12 beer in six-liter bottles with the intention to vintage them. The vintage process of a premium beer means paying for it, storing it, caring for it, and then selling it two or more years down the road. "That is a sign of long-term commitment," effuses the beer professional.

Dave Blanchard considers his Belgian cooler with partner Tom Moore

Yes, the Brick Store boys are committed with a capital "C." Take a look at their current project to build a beer cellar located underneath the Square in an old bank vault. Although in the rough development stage at the time of this writing, the vault is already making sensational waves with industry professionals. Claus Hagelman, national sales manager for Dogfish Head Craft Brewery, got a peek while scoping out a Georgia distributor. As he walked around downstairs feeling at home with his pint, Claus next wandered upstairs and to the left into the Belgian Bar. It was here that he knew a great old school beer geek mind was at work—that is until he tagged alone with Dave downstairs into the cellar. Claus' reaction: "Wow! Those are the days I love being in this business. I have often thought of getting off the road and opening a bar myself, and if I did I would copy The Brick Store." Everyone in the craft beer industry had a first great spot where they learned to love beer, study the styles, and discover some favorites. Claus reflects that, "These places were our homes, our schools, and almost our church. The first time I entered the Brick Store I knew this was one of those magical places."

Sam Calagione, Dogfish Head founder and president, also remembers ambling through the bank vault full of old dusty bottles. Blown away by the expansive, well-curated vintage beer stash, Sam loved that all this excellence was happening in such a warm, friendly, unpretentious environment. "Everyone who works there exudes beer passion without beer snobbery." As someone who prefers to keep his place a bit whacky and unconventional, Sam's Dogfish dream are described by beer writer Michael Jackson as: "America's most interesting and adventurous small brewery." If that's not a kissing cousin of the Pub, then nothing is.

Dennis Lange, proprietor of the independent 5 Seasons Brewing restaurants in metro Atlanta, shares a mutually supportive relationship with the Pub boys (with a healthy dose of merciless teasing). As a brewer, he is thrilled to see another establishment that thrives on cutting edge experimentation. "That's where the peanut butter hits the chocolate," jokes Dennis. As he looks up and around the Pub's high ceiling, Dennis reflects on the Brick Store's accomplishments as well as his own entrepreneurial path through the words of Henry David Thoreau, namely that most men live a life of quiet desperation. Or in the words of Mr. Lange, "If you're not the lead dog, you're following and always sniffing butt somewhere."

So many can't see the forest for the trees, it seems. No matter, as Dave, Mike, and Tom ignored every person who told them that their business model was insane or that they could make way more money if they tried. Classic car mechanic and Brick Store staple Neil Estes lets out a guffaw at the memory of one such blind man. It came during the Pub's first month when the bar was packed elbow-to-elbow. A pal of his had ordered a Miller Lite only to be informed of the policy and balked, swearing incredulously, "That's the craziest thing I've ever heard. This place will never make it!" Sure, Neil chuckled to himself as he squeezed through the massive crowd, "Yeah, they'll never make it." He, too, has been called an anomaly in the niche of classic cars. Neil's Restoration has established a reputation for straight dealing and a focus on cars before anything else (similar things said about the Brick Store).

Rob Tod of Allagash Brewing Company looks at making beer through the eyes of an artist as if he was painting or arranging music. While the monetary rewards are far from huge, the satisfaction in creating something unique keeps his outfit running strong. Rob's team at Allagash love brewing beer, work hard to do so consistently, and vibe strongly with the company's mission and vision. "We are not money or volume driven, so anyone who comes into our environment without the passion for or dedication to making craft beer just doesn't last." It was the founder's pleasure to attend the Brick Store's Allagash beer dinner and soak in the south as one of the next big growth segments for craft beer. As Rob looked into Dave's eyes, he saw the same satisfaction in creating an environment to display these labors of love. "They [Brick Store owners] love these beers. They are *the* venue and they get to present an opportunity for people to have a beer experience like they've never had."

> **Witbier (Allagash White):** A Belgian style ale that's very pale and cloudy in appearance due to it being unfiltered as well as the high level of wheat, and sometimes oats that are used in the mash. Always spiced, generally with coriander, orange peel, and other oddball spices or herbs in the background. The crispness and slight twang of the witbier come from the wheat and the lively level of carbonation. This is one style that many brewers in the U.S. have taken a liking to, and they have done a very good job of staying true to its style. Sometimes served with a lemon, if you truly want to enjoy the untainted subtleties of this style you'll ask for yours without one. Often referred to as "white beers" (witbieren) due to the cloudiness/ yeast in suspension.

It takes grit and grace to own and run a world-class drinking establishment. For anyone who yearns to enter the race, here are six mile markers to meet along the journey. Some are obvious, others are subtle—and a few are downright mystical.

Cultivate Your Clientele's Palate

The Brick Store founders opened their doors with a humble and profound vision of the sort on which the American Dream is made: first, to own and operate their own neighborhood pub. Second, to go against the grain of what every other bar on the planet was doing. No TVs, no neon lighting, no gimmicks, no specials, no beer-of-the-month club, no light or domestic beer. With guts, intention, and ignorance, the young lads grabbed a hold of sledgehammers and manifested their dream. What they built was an authentic and stellar pub atmosphere whose character spoke for itself. "You had me at hello," gushed an early patron.

Although the Brick Store of today rules the niche of premier beer bar, it was not that way in the beginning. The Pub's focus and expertise grew organically over time as the three new entrepreneurs cultivated their business skills and tended their vision. "We had all managed a bar, but none of us had owned our own place. As our own knowledge and experience raised around beer, so did that of our customers," explains Mike Gallagher. Still, from day one, the guys knew what the Pub was, namely a unique and spectacular drinking establishment. Thus they constantly nurtured opportunities to expand their customers' imbibing habits.

Case in point was Warsteiner, the Pub's former high standard German pilsner that served a faithful eight years as the bartenders' go-to selection for the question, "Do you have Miller Lite on draught?" Far from a "starter beer," and enjoying its own rightful following (especially after softball games), this fine German brew stood as the only thing fractionally close to a traditional domestic on the menu. Visiting fathers, uncles, and brothers who professed themselves light beer drinkers quickly became amenable to this foreign sounding beverage, their perplexing looks melting into gratitude and relief nine times out of ten.

Despite its beautiful golden color and even served in a proper glass mug, Warsteiner still swallowed hard for those accustomed to Coors. The Pub's commitment to beer education and offering new standards for American palates overcame the reluctance, however. The vast majority of patrons became willing to surrender their skepticism on top of that horseshoe bar like a holy altar.

Then came a shocking day in 2005 when the Warsteiner got pulled off draught. Devotees felt as sad as if their sports team had just been sold. Most of us take to change like a cat takes to a bathtub full of water, yet the miracle workers of the Brick Store soothed the disappointment graciously. With patience and confidence, bartenders and servers soon had everyone on board with its replacement, namely the top-rated Victory Prima Pils. Only the finest pilsner made in the United States, this pilsner was once referred by another craft industry brewer as "my island beer" (you know, the one beer you would take with you if shipwrecked). The "lighter" beer regulars hung on like champs and now they sing songs praising Prima Pils.

> **Pilsner** (Victory Prima Pils): First brewed in Bohemia, a German-speaking province in the old Austrian Empire, this is the most popular style of lager in Germany and many other countries. Often spelled "pilsener," abbreviated, or spoken in slang, as "pils," it ranges from a very light straw to golden in color. It has a dense and rich head. It is well-hopped using noble hops. It exhibits a spicy herbal or floral aroma and flavor, and is often a bit coarse on the palate. It can distribute a flash of citrus-like zest. The hop bitterness can be high.

Over the course of a decade, the Pub converted thousands of ordinary consumers' mindsets from *what beer is* to *what beer could be*. As one patron survey reported, "I came in two days after it opened because I wanted a good beer. I started on A and am on about L." Customers in those early years who resisted the freshness of the Pub's approach simply weeded themselves out and went to a different watering hole of their liking. It was a win-win for all. Now the Brick Store is considered the gold standard in customer education.

An important distinction in the area of beer knowledge is how the Brick Store transcends facts and instead gets to the heart of an imbibing experience. "Although passion for beer in and of themselves are a great place to start, I think the most important thing is being excited about *sharing* beer and beer knowledge with other folks. Otherwise, where's the fun in it?" says Pub owner Michael Gallagher. His attitude reveals the entrepreneurial magical of such an establishment. "It's a privilege that we know as much as we do about delicious craft beer and we strive to be gracious in sharing that with our guests and making them feel welcome."

A stellar example of taking the time to cultivate palates comes from bar manager Ryan Gallagher and a certain client who walked in the Pub one day looking for a Bud Light. "Well, we don't carry that, sir," Ryan stated. He remembers the disappointment in the man's face and how much he wanted that beer. By his appearance, it was obvious that this guest had just put in a long, hard day of blue collar work. He probably hoped for nothing more in that moment than his usual cold brew and his current barstool. Ryan took a breath and got down to business: "Look there's something I can start you off with, it's refreshing…try this Prima Pils." After a pregnant pause, the laborer agreed to give it a try.

As he walked through the restaurant, Ryan noticed that the man was now nurturing a second draught and checked in. Looking fairly happy, he offered Ryan a half-grinned response of "It's not too bad." Ryan joked with his guest that he'd be drinking Guinness before too long. Four months passed before the bar manager saw his student again. Ryan proudly chuckles when describing their next encounter: "I walked into the Brick Store and there he is waving to me from the bar with a (dark, malty, strong) Lagunitas Lumpy Gravy in his hand shouting, 'I made it!'" It was a beer graduation worthy of a diploma.

> **American Brown Ale** (Lagunitas Lumpy Gravy): Spawned from the English Brown Ale using American ingredients this style also encompasses "dark ales." These have a wide range of bitterness and hop flavor, as well as varying alcohol contents.

Serve Beer in Proper Glassware and at the Correct Temperature

Craft beer engages all the senses. Its color ranges widely from black to copper to gold to pink, making it a banquet feast for the eyes. Aromas fill the nostrils: notes of citrus, hops, chocolate, and more. It lands on the palate with flavor tastes as expected as malt and as wild as asparagus. Drinking it can incorporate the sounds of popping corks and rolling bottles (done to mix the yeast sediment back into the brew), which are a delight to the ears. The touch of a beer bottle that came from a small brewery, or maybe crossed an ocean, feels good in your hand, as you let a frothy beer head dance in your mouth.

Finally, craft beer engages the sixth sense of intuition. You know when you are drinking something special, like a Dupont Moinette Brune. One sip of this Belgian strong ale, with its superb yeast balance, and you feel as if you just tasted fresh baked bread. But wait, are you in the Belgian Bar anymore or were you instantly transported to your mom's kitchen where there's a hearty loaf coming out of the oven? Or are you on European holiday, out on a cobblestone street early in the day, where you've just taken your first bite of a warm baguette? Did your palate just genuflect in a Trappist chapel?

The magic of really good beer (and all superior food and beverages) is that your body knows the truth even if your head doesn't understand the science. For the record, a Moinette Brune leaves your mouth refreshed with a clean, dry finish after it crosses your tongue. Furthermore, the composition of Belgian beer is singular in its ability to marry yeast levels with a perfect balance of fruit strands and carbonation levels. But it's never about the facts alone. Instead, sit back, relax, and enjoy each sip.

Belgian Strong Dark Ale (Moinette Brune): Similar to Belgian Dark Ale, but higher in alcohol with more all-around character. Alcohol can be deceivingly hidden or very bold and in your face. There is lots of complexity within a delicate palate. It has varying hop and malt character. Most are fruity, spicy, and alcoholic and may have mild dark malt flavors. Phenols range from minimal to high.

Born in the brewery with vision and passion, these little labors of love are deserving of the best treatment possible until they reach the lips of a reverent public. There's just one word to describe stale beer: gross. It tastes like paper or, worse, has no taste at all. As for getting your beer served in a frozen mug, well, ice crystals might go well with American fizzy-water but they are flat-out offensive to a handcrafted beer. Imagine this: it's the Fourth of July in an American bar and you've ordered yourself a Chimay Red (your patriotic plan being to next savor a Chimay White and then a Chimay Blue). Your authentic, monastic beverage arrives in a cold mug with a mega-beer brand name emblazoned on the pint glass. To top it off, the glass also carries a St. Patrick's Day logo. This isn't just tacky, it's heresy. Yet this happens in bars all over North America. Free glassware from distributors and breweries mean saving a buck, but at a serious price to the integrity our beverages and our imbibing experience.

Enter the beer oasis of the Southeast, the Brick Store Pub, where the exact opposite is true. This is a place where an *entire room* is dedicated to proper glassware. Over 70 percent of all beer served at the Pub comes in the glass meant for that style and brand alone. From a chunky, indestructible Westmalle goblet to the most fragile of all, a Huyghe Kira white glass, the gourmet beers of the Brick Store are delivered to your seat in elegance and style. After all, Trappist monks did not perform a literal act of God for you to receive a final presentation that's anything less than sacred. They drink out of chalices, for heaven's sake!

A proper glass is designed to honor and advance the beer drinking experience. It is engineered so that you are hit in the nose with a craft beer's rich aroma and so that your eyes may feast on its beautiful shades and hues. Take, for example, the German Ayinger Celebrator Doppelbock (sounds entrancing from the start). Because it comes in an 11.2-ounce bottle, the Celebrator glass is seven inches high and three inches wide at the rim, the exact right dimension to show off its dark ruby brown color and release wafts of its earthy fruit smell. Move to a Weihenstephaner, possibly the finest representation of a hefe weizen on Earth, and the glass becomes tall and narrow in order to fully display a fluffy white head of foam. Delve a bit deeper into the German design and you discover how pretty the cloudy wheat grist haze becomes when held up to the light (it sure as heck isn't to encourage sippy straw use). Less surface area also keeps in carbonation and retains the wheat beer effervescence—longhand for yum.

Hefeweizen (Weihenstephaner): A southern German style of wheat beer (weissbier) made with a typical ratio of 50:50 wheat to yeast. "Hefe" means "with yeast." Yeast produces a unique phenolic flavor of banana and cloves, with an often dry and tart edge, as well as some spiciness, bubblegum, or notes of apples. Yeast produces an unfiltered, cloudy appearance. It has little hop bitterness and moderate levels of alcohol. Sexy when poured into a traditional Weizen glass, it is often served with a lemon wedge (popularized by Americans) to cut its wheat or yeast edge. This is a flavorful snap for some and an insult for others (damaging taste and head retention).

In a day and age where beer drinking ascends to new heights, settling for bland glassware is boring. Instead there's opportunity for pure Belgian romance by the decree of Trappist ale chalice presentation. Open and wide-rimmed at the top, Belgian goblets accentuate the color and aroma of the beer, and allow for a quick dissipating head of these historic, heavily carbonated recipes. The result is a classic spider web-like "Belgian lace" that sticks to the chalice walls. This effect is akin to the "legs" on a finely made wine. Surely those blessed boys at the Abbey of Saint Benedict would appreciate the efforts of the Brick Store to serve a slice of heaven (like their Achel Blonde) in its proper glass.

You don't have to be a holy roller either, as all deserving beers are venerated at the Brick Store. Even Lucifer gets proper treatment, as evidenced by the Pub's efforts to stock Duvel goblets. This Flemish family-owned brewery may be named for the devil (in Dutch Brabantian), however their products attest that they are well versed in all things devotional. Look at how they celebrate fermentation, namely by carving a large "D" in the bottom of their Duvel glass to collect carbonation. When the bubbles come off that etched D, *WHOOSH*, they shoot up the side like a tornado and create almost half a glass of head. The experience is miraculous enough to convert thee of little faith, if only for a spell in Decatur's Belgian Bar.

As common sense dictates, beer quantity does not automatically denote quality. Buyers should beware of bars that carry a draught and bottle selection in the hundreds but slacks on maintaining their lines and rotating their selections. Better to have an incredible, yet not overwhelming beer list than to have your fermented enjoyment travel for miles, sit stale in the lines, and arrive through the tap in a sub par manner. Imagine laying down your well-earned coinage only to scrunch up your nose at an off-tasting beer, shafted by a cheap close-out artist, who bought the keg close to expiration date for the sake of a deal. Suffice it to say, this would never happen at the Pub where the managers care deeply about the brew quality, and they know coming in the door if it's not right. If something appears wrong, the tap handle gets pulled immediately. End of story.

Impeccably maintained, top-rated industry tap lines are another must if you want to deliver the freshest beer possible. Still a wish-list item for many restaurants, the Brick Store stepped up and installed the best equipment available a few years into their opening. Now the downstairs main bar and Belgian Bar taps each stay on their own CO_2 regulators, producing less waste and a better drinking experience for the customer.

Forget the engineering for a second, instead let's look at the gorgeous, curvy figures of those main bar beer taps. These smooth, large uniform handles gleam a beautiful sea green in the afternoon skylight sun, their aesthetically pleasing, coaster-round branded logos sitting atop like tempting lollipops. "I'll take a ruby red, an orange, a golden and, um, a tan," the adults ask eagerly at the downstairs counter. Skippity-skip goes the Brick Store vibe.

From the bar side, the evolution of branded glassware looked like bunnies multiplying—one day they unlocked the Pub door and stemware was everywhere. An accurate exaggeration, the proliferation deemed it necessary to build some glass bunny pens and fast. Extra shelving got wrapped above the Belgian Bar and beneath the downstairs main bar. Out went all items that weren't nailed down in the old storage closet so it could be transformed to the glassware room. Thus Dave began spending his days juggling fragile beer steins, flutes, goblets, and willibeckers.

If you are in Germany or Belgium, it is simply customary to have your beverage a proper glass. They wouldn't have it any other way at the Pub. As Dave puts it plainly about carrying and stocking so many unwieldy glasses, "It's what we do." They even hired a dishwasher.

Remembering their unique vision from day one, Dave continues: "Originally we were pouring pilsner in pilsner glasses, wheat in wheat glasses, and ales in ale glasses. It was generic, however we were serving it properly and nobody else was. We did not serve pitchers of beer. We actually carried imperial pints. We had the right beer in the right glasses before anyone else—and that's for certain."

Evident striving for excellence is summed up nicely by a typical review on BeerAdvocate.com:

> *The selection is insane: Things on tap that you couldn't get just anywhere. Bud-what? I had the fish and chips with the Reinsdorf Kölsch and a St. Bernardus Alt 12 quadruple. The beers were served in exactly the right glass (who the*

hell has Kölsch glasses?). If I were building a pub, this is the blueprint.

> **Kölsch** (Reinsdorf): First only brewed in Köln, Germany, now many American brewpubs and a handful of breweries have created their own version of this obscure style. Light to medium in body with a very pale color, the hop bitterness is medium to slightly assertive. A somewhat vinous (grape-y from malts) and dry flavor makes up the rest.

The whole glassware affair started back in the early 2000s with LaTrappe, a high octane Belgian ale that you could only get one place in all of metro Atlanta, the Brick Store Pub. For a good stretch, the Pub reigned as the number one LaTrappe account in the United States, draining four kegs a week for thirsty beer geeks who drove sixty miles round trip from Alpharetta to taste a sip of this cult brew. Its mystique grew as the Pub served the Trappist beer properly in a chalice, the only glass of its kind in the house. Everyone wanted to know what draught was travelling to their neighbor's table in that special looking glass. "Can I have one of those?" As chalice fever caught through the Pub, the guys took serious note as to the power of authentic stemware.

"Proper glassware became viral within the Brick Store walls, and it spread to other Atlanta bar managers and beyond," says Philip Jarrell, former sales rep for (defunct) Thunderhead Distribution. He would know as he was the man responsible for bringing all those LaTrappe kegs into the Pub. Philip holds the highest esteem for Dave, Mike, and Tom not only for their boldness in serving beer properly, but also for going the distance in their business to change the homogenization of beer culture. "They were the forefathers of the correct beer movement in Atlanta," attests Philip.

Treat Your Staff with Consummate Respect

Fastidious drink presentation would fall upon "deaf palates" were it not for committed servers and bartenders who carry out the Brick Store's vision and mission as if they built the place themselves. This all-star staff is a huge reason as to why we nearly levitate while sipping our imperial pints in the Pub. Likewise, an earned reputation as a top world beer establishment is hand in hand with consistent, friendly, knowledgeable service. Remember, this is not pouring ordinary liquids into average containers. This is passion that shows. As a visiting German commented on his bar service, "How can I transport that back to my country?"

Always relaxed, even when slammed on a weekday night, the bartenders and servers at the Pub appear to read minds when it comes to recommending beer. Because the drink list rivals a foreign tourist map, some patrons feel downright intimidated leafing through the large selection, stammering out a feeble plea for help, "I just have no idea what I want. Can you suggest something?"

"What do you usually drink?" lobs the confident bartender to the flabbergasted customer. If she gets no response, another soft pitch is thrown: "Are you into darker beer, light, sweet, hoppy?" Based on a mixture of that response, some ESP, today's newest arrivals and the server's personal favorites, a beer magically appears on the bar. Wide-eyed that the perfect pint was yielded from such little information, "Oh, how did you know?" the guest says, as he sits back and sighs pleasantly, ready for a relaxed and interesting drinking session at the Brick Store. Given the vastness of the drink menu, the service goes beyond being professional. It's all out impressive.

Now please don't waltz into the Brick Store and expect a mini-symposium from your server on how beer is made or the difference between tripel and quadrupel Belgian ale, the current price and availability of hops in America, or any other such thing. Beer geekness is much appreciated at the Pub, however these kids are busy and their number one concern is getting some drinks on your table—and fast. What's more, no server is required to be a walking beer encyclopedia (although one or more are always about). Conversely, you can rest assured that staff could not and would not fake a beer recommendation. It doesn't take long to pick up what's what on tap or in the cooler, and besides the owners encourage sampling. "Someone new would get it by osmosis alone," says Dave.

It may appear that savvy servers pull back the veil to simply reveal the mysteries of handcrafted beer, but their aim is to draw you into the process. This level of dedication caught the attention of Steve German, a sales rep from Pennsylvania-based Victory Brewing Company, whose gold standard for any establishment is the service of the bartenders.

As an industry veteran, Steve has sat at countless bar stools for business. However, he always arrives unannounced at first so he can form his own opinion as if he were an unassuming customer. When Steve first sat at the Brick Store's horseshoe bar and asked for a beer suggestion, he received a question back, "What do you like," followed by an offer to match his tastes preferences. This was instant proof that the Brick Store's accolades for knowledgeable staff were on the money.

Steve had to wait for a return visit to test the Pub on his next gold standard, namely a bartender remembering his name. Not only did the staff meet the sales rep's muster, a waitress stopped him outside the door as he was leaving. "Hey, you're Steve, right? I worked for you two years ago as a server for your beer dinner. That was a great night. We love Victory Prima Pils. Bye, now!"

Steve's next observation of greatness alludes to a subtle magnetic factor that makes Pub life so alluring. For when he entered through the wooden door, Steve immediately noticed "all the ink" on the staff including a full tattoo ink sleeve on the bartender's arm (Arch Woodard). "While I am not tattooed," says the mild mannered professional, "I look at this culture as a whole and I see that this is a person committed to something. And then when I see that culture in a bar, and I get a question [about my tastes] instead of somebody's opinion…that was the first time I knew the Brick Store was a class joint."

Why is this comment remotely significant? Outward appearances such as tattoos, piercings, and mohawks can elicit reactions from instant bonding and admiration to a complete put off and everything in between. Many employers would rather play it safe and keep their staff as uniform and clean cut in appearance as possible with a "check your personality at the door" type attitude. Yet a major factor in the Pub's authenticity and good vibe is the cumulative effect of self-expression and no employee uniforms. In contrast to a homogeneous cotton shirt, server personality is allowed to shine through a come-as-you-are dress policy—albeit clean, neat, and no bare midriffs.

Grateful, the bartenders show up in their Virgin of Guadalupe and skate boarding tee shirts, fisherman caps and fedoras, mini-skirts and ankle-length vintage wraps. Dreadlocks fly free and tattoos are on proud display. This allowance, underrated by many restaurant owners, puts an invisible spring in the step of these most human of beings. If servers and bartenders are going to work long hours and wait on (sometimes very tipsy) people for tips, at least they're wearing their real clothes and being their true selves. It's a level of respect that keeps the job applications stacked high and the employee turnover rate running low (very low).

Belgian Bar Boys: Bartenders Bryan, Matt, Miles, and Jesse

Back to Steve German, the straight-laced, fifty-something, admittedly reserved, Irish-American male who isn't a stick in the mud, but is a far cry from a motorcycle riding film character from *Easy Rider*. He is not the only person to have an initial slight disconnect between tattooed skin and outstanding service in a renowned establishment such as the Brick Store. The fact that he overcame this bias underscores the overall nature of the Pub as a melting pot, a welcoming place where human assumptions regarding class, creed, and culture are invited to melt away for the sake of fellowship and great pints—on either side of the bar.

For the record, there is no counterculture mandate at the Brick Store. None of the owners have branded skin and many staff look as everyday as the English professors, nursing students, and psychology doctoral candidates that they are. It just so happens that the Pub has evolved into one of those precious rare working environments where song of the soul is as prominent as professionalism. Oh what a difference that makes!

In reality, it's not a walk in the park to consistently hit the high notes of beer presentation along with guest satisfaction in casual pub dining. With all this stinking special glassware and long lists for properly handling the beer, you might think the staff gets a bit, well, cranky lugging heavy trays in a packed restaurant night after night. The short answer is yes, they get tired. It's worth the effort, however. Although the owners are persnickety about their glassware at the Pub, so is the long lost art of employer empathy and respect.

When it comes to a restaurant, employee functionality is often considered an act of grace rather than a given. Skipping the dissertation on why (go read a chapter of *Kitchen Confidential* by Anthony Bourdain), suffice it to say the Brick Store emanates a thankful harmony among cooks, servers, bartenders, managers, and owners. It's really, really simple when it comes to respect at the Pub. The guys always put themselves in the place of their staff and act accordingly. As one bartender puts it, "The bosses treat you the same way as you treat your friends."

Whether that's going the extra mile to honor requests for days off, or giving the cooks a shot of whiskey after a pummeling Decatur festival shift (there are a whopping five different annual festivals held on the Square), these owners are in serious touch with the grueling side of working in a restaurant. If there's a task to perform that stretches employee dignity, the guys don't schlep it off. They do it themselves or hire outside help. "I've never worked in a place where I was treated with more dignity," says cook Paul Pietschner.

Because they go to such great lengths at developing their internal culture and treating their staff well, the guys loathe firing someone. "We sweat it out for two days if we have to have *the talk* with an employee," they share. One bartender who had that talk begged for his job and shifted his attitude because he knew how good he had it. "Thank you for granting me some amnesty," the poet spoke at a Brick Store party. Another loquacious server knew he wasn't a speed devil around the Pub and so did his three bosses. So he took the lead during their annual one-on-one employee chat by presenting his best asset, personality: "First, let me apologize for the fact that I'm Gerg. Next, let's celebrate that fact!" (It worked, the guys died with laughter). Yet another staff member, nicknamed "Server McWorsty" for his flagrant laxness, shook his head gratefully during his book interview and with a teary-eye said, "I've been treated better here than I feel I deserve."

Pittsburg native and manager Lee Dickson first read about the Belgian Bar on BeerAdvocate.com and made a special trip to Decatur for his brother's twenty-first birthday. After popping some vintage bottles with Dave, Lee kept in touch over email, eventually moving to Atlanta with his wife. A huge beer connoisseur, Lee hungered for a job at the Pub and spoke with all three owners for over two hours about it. "We just don't have room for you, but we like you. Stick around." Lee came to the bar every day and brought in special beer until a server position opened up. During his formal interview, he sat in a chair facing the three men and felt relaxed as opposed to intimidated, as he knew it was ultimately up to him. "They do a great job with letting you decide for yourself if you fit in," shares Lee. Scowling at the memory, the manager remembers a job where he only saw his boss sit down twice with a beer in hand over a span of five years. "It's not like that here," Lee asserts. "Dave, Mike, and Tom build personal relationships. I would never want to take advantage of them."

Industry representative Adrianna Jarrell of Georgia Crown echoes these sentiments, commenting that she never hears complaints in the field about the Brick Store. "It's a *functional* family," she says of her top-tier client and number one Weihenstephaner account. Adrianna senses the caring employer-employee rapport through the way she is treated by the staff who always offer her coffee and call her by name.

> *"They work their butts off, and we appreciate that. We always tip well. You'd have to pay me a lot to work like that all night."*
>
> —Brenda Thames, Javamonkey
> Speaks poetry regular

"Other clients, well, you're just a thought to them when they need something, very old school that makes me wonder how they treat their staff." Bars are her work environment, thus Adrianna is keen on respectful, symbiotic relationships where both parties benefit. What it's all about for this professional is how she is treated by a buyer. "That's where I spend my own money, and I have no problem spending it at the Brick Store Pub."

Employees love spending their money at the Pub too, as let's not forget how fun it is to work in America's number two rated beer bar. A generous employee discount policy allows for a healthy sampling of all the craft beer that is sold at the Pub. It's a privilege greatly exercised. On any given day there is an after-work gathering of staff kicking back at an outside neighboring table soaking each other's essence and drinking big, bold, delicious beers. The most recent and most long running staff favorite is undeniably the sublime St. Bernardus Abt. 12 stated on the menu as "a truly wonderful beer." One bartender dreamily describes the experience of drinking this strong, creamy Trappist ale as "curling up in front of a fireplace," even if it's the month of August. Perhaps this is why Darius of D&V International has to "keep a substantial amount of these kegs on hand just for Dave."

Belgian Quadrupel (St. Bernardus Abt. 12): A Trappist inspired ale of great strength with a bolder flavor than its dubbel and tripel sister styles. Typically a dark creation ranging within deep red, brown, and garnet hues, a "Quad" has a full-bodied, rich malty palate. It contains moderate levels of phenols. It is sweet with a low bitterness yet a well perceived alcohol.

The bottom line regarding employer respect is spoken well by local photographer and Pub regular Hector Amador: "Thank you for treating your staff so well. They all act like the owners. They all act like they are happy to see you at their place."

Push the Envelope I: The Georgia Beer Laws Change

"Upstairs and to the left." That's the quick answer given by bartenders and servers when asked the whereabouts of the well-hidden, magnificent Brick Store Belgian Bar. Its entranceway barely noticeable from the top of the Pub stairs, the Belgian Bar's low ceiling joists, brick archway, and cozy corners makes it feel like a basement tavern in Amsterdam. "But on the second floor, only in America," comments a visiting German who has never seen such a thing. This gourmet beer haven exudes so much old world charm that it easily could have its own underground secret knock if set in another time period. Some long time patrons still haven't discovered it.

The near tragedy is that it almost never existed. For a very long time, you couldn't legally buy or sell a beer in Georgia that was over 6.0 percent ABV. The only way to get your hands on one was to brew a batch in your garage or to mail order it from across state lines. That made building a Belgian Bar moot, since Abbey ales are typically much higher in alcohol content. Who were they going to serve up there, crickets?

Then came the blessed "cap popping" day in 2004 when an amended law got put on state record that allowed for beer sales up to 14 percent ABV. This came about thanks to the monumental efforts of Georgians for World Class Beer (GWCB), a committed alliance of citizens, beer enthusiasts, and industry professionals who worked tirelessly to ensure the availability of outstanding American and imported craft beer.

Before we dive into the larger story of GWCB and the birth of the Belgian Bar, a history lesson is in order. The background of American hand crafted beer is a tale tenacious of creative passion. All throughout our country's young history, new world brewers made concoctions surging with the flavor of old-world recipes. That is until the thirteen years of Prohibition (ending in 1933) when alcohol was banned and microbreweries bit the dust in massive numbers. When U.S. beer production resumed, it was at an industrial level—mass-produced varieties with little character, tradition, or taste.

Then Fritz Maytag (of home appliance fame) bought the old Anchor Brewing Company in 1965. The revival of this San Francisco microbrewery served as a lighthouse for fledgling independents. With solid leadership in place, other American brew enthusiasts bravely opened shop in fits and spurts over the next two decades. The new wave of pioneers kept on brewing through the 70s and 80s, largely ignored by the general industry. Then suddenly in the 1990s the small batch beer movement exploded and micro-produced beverages spilled heavily into the market scene.

Independents started reaping major "wheat" as their beers got swept up by a drinking populace that was parched for flavor and innovation. These micro-offerings slaked an enormous consumer thirst for beer that tasted different and was crafted in the new tradition.. Well, new by American standards, although brewers once again drew from long-standing European techniques that used an increased weight of sugars (derived from malted barley or sometimes candie sugar), that produced a "high gravity" beer.

Gravity in the sense of beer making has nothing to do with an apple falling on your head by the laws of Newton. Instead, gravity is a term used to measure the percentage of sugar (alcohol) in a beer after it is done brewing. The unit of measuring sugar is called a "unit Plato" (°P), named for a German chemist. So how do you estimate the units Plato of a beer? Well, imagine you're standing over a big, hot vat of ingredients. Before the fermentation process, you take a device called a hydrometer (like a thermometer) and measure the alcohol content or the "original gravity." After the beer is finished fermenting, you measure the alcohol content again or the "finishing gravity." If the resulting product is over seven °P, it's considered to be a "high gravity" beer by industry standards.

Don't worry if you barely passed chemistry class, all you need to know is that "high gravity" means a specialty craft beer that is higher in alcohol because it contains more sugar and other ingredients at the start of the brewing process (more ingredients = more sugar = more alcohol = way more flavor). See, a craft beer brewer is part chemist, part artist who follows her heart's desire when she is creating a complex, flavorful liquid. Because she wants the freedom to add any ingredient her intuition or imagination deems necessary, this gal reserves the right to use as much sugar as she pleases to balance the whole vat out and make her beer taste dandy and delicious (and you thought chocolate was a girl's best friend).

Why is this history and science lesson important? You deserve to understand that craft beer is as American as apple pie and high gravity beers are brewed for maximum flavor unchained by ABV laws. There's no adolescent intent behind brewing a high alcohol beer. These babies are meant for adult sipping and leisurely doting.

"He was a wise man who invented beer."

—Plato

Georgia legislators heard not a word of this discussion, however. When GWCB first showed up at the state capitol building in 2000 parading their fancy, high gravity ideas, they might as well have been speaking the tongue of the devil. For it all boiled down to the only two words conservative lawmakers heard: *higher alcohol.* No one cared a whit about taste, connoisseurship, or supposed fairness to beer consumers. Increased alcohol content meant one thing to elected officials—drunk kids. The idea went nowhere fast for two years without becoming an officially written bill.

GWCB, spearheaded by beer enthusiasts Ted Hull and Mark Nelson, was ready for an influx of heavy lifters by 2002. Industry professionals Rob Nelson and Pete Martee answered the call and smartly approached a Decatur legislator to sponsor a bill. They asked Georgia House Representative Stephanie Stuckey Benfield, a lawyer, mother of two, and longtime Brick Store Pub fan. Rep. Benfield became quite familiar with the ethics and values of the Brick Store's culture when her law office sat right off the Decatur Square. She clearly understood the proposal for what it meant—quality, reverent imbibing—and became the bill's champion.

Dave Blanchard had been watching from the sidelines for most of this time, honing his proprietor chops and tending his Pub. Like his business partners, Dave traveled often and paid attention to cutting edge trends. The beer bar visionary saw the writing on the wall of craft beer's emergence as the next big thing in the food and beer world. As GWCB chugged along, he caught sight of what the Brick Store could become—the "best beer bar" in Atlanta.

Mind you, the Pub already was sitting on top of a mound of local accolades, an existing preeminent beer selection, and a golden-child aura. Dave Blanchard could have sat back, done nothing, and still been an owner of one of Georgia's top bars. But that is the antithesis of this man's nature. As Dave talked up the idea of expanding their bar to his partners, all three owners understood this as a high risk venture. Yet there was greater risk of saying no and letting the opportunity pass them by. Besides, beer was their passionate love. The boys mustered the will and made their move to join the fray happening down in the halls of the State Legislature.

Their active presence turned the tide from GWCB as a "shoestring operation" to a legitimate group of influence. A professional lobbyist was hired thanks to beer dinner fundraisers held at the Pub and 5 Seasons Brewery, as well as funds appropriated from the Great Decatur Beer Festival. Thankfully, Ronnie Chance agreed to come on board for only a fraction of his normal lobbyist fees. After two years of getting shot down in the House, the gourmet beer bill became primed for passing.

Dave, Mike, and others trucked down to join Ronnie in educating lawmakers on the issue as both a connoisseur's market and increased tax revenue. They put an Orval bottle right into a representative's hand to impress upon him the difference between an indulgent Belgian four-pack that cost ten dollars versus a cheap twenty-four domestic suitcase that cost a little over thirteen bucks. Then they'd ask him, "If you were a broke college kid, which would you pick?"

Slowly the rhetoric sunk in. As the bill got re-written to match the Georgia wine laws, GWCB watched their body of support grow. More and more folks began contacting their local legislators. An email went out every time another lawmaker came on board, bringing folks together in the Decatur Square parking lot to shout, "Yes! We won one more over tonight!" It was an exciting and memorable time for Georgia beer lovers.

And then it finally happened. In early January, just two weeks into the 2004 legislative session, the bill was passed and Georgia joined well over forty other states in making gourmet beers available to the public. It was a watershed moment for the entire beer community, especially at the Brick Store. On July 1, 2004, the new state law officially started and residents lined up outside the Pub's door and around the Decatur Square to celebrate their first sip of higher ABV beer on Georgia's "Beer Independence Day." A new era had begun.

Trappist Breweries

Did you know there are only seven official Trappist breweries? Six are Belgian and one is Dutch:

Achel	Westmalle
Chimay	Westvleteren
Orval	Koningshoeven (Dutch)
Rochefort	

To carry the Authentic Trappist Product logo, three criteria must be met:

*The beer must be brewed within the walls of a Trappist abbey (or brewing controlled by Trappist monks)

*The brewery must be owned and operated by the monastic community

*The economic purpose of the brewery must be for charity and not profit

Push the Envelope II: The Birth of the Belgian Bar

As Georgia became open territory for the niche market of handcrafted beer, a bevy of breweries, brokers, and distributors came calling over the next year. Sales reps poured into the bar scene with microbrew samples as if it were the 1850's California Gold Rush. Discovering a potential account such as the Brick Store Pub must have felt like striking it rich. For here was beer utopia: a well-intentioned environment with tons of character, impeccable top-of-the-line equipment, a thoroughly knowledgeable staff, a cultivated clientele, and owners whose enthusiasm and excitement exceeded their own. Here was an *entire* space dedicated to Belgian ale. Brokers probably half-expected a McChoffe gnome to start talking or a monk to stumble out of the cooler in a state of meditative bliss.

Yet the conception of the Belgian Bar came from a humble and practical question: where were the guys going to stock the hundreds of independent high gravity beers that would soon be coming their way (and eager to serve)? There's only so much room in any house, and the Brick Store was already close to beer cooler capacity before the law changes. Once Georgia popped the ABV cap in January, it literally came down to expanding their current location or opening a second bar.

The Pub's landlord, next door neighbor Glen Gurevich of Sweet Melissa's, rarely used the 800-square foot second floor of his restaurant. Once upon a time he sold pizzas out of there and occasionally Glen rented it out for parties. Otherwise, it served as storage space or a break room for his kitchen and wait staff. Many moons earlier, Glen had told his tenants that if they wanted to hash out an idea regarding expansion, they knew where to find him. Of course, it would have to make sense for all of them and the timing had to be right.

The spring of 2004, it made sense and the timing was right. Dave came knocking.

What started as a simple notion for more beer cooler space grew into a full-fledged master plan for the Belgian Bar. In May, Dave got the ball rolling by hiring an inspector, getting a permit, and soliciting the opinion of his older brother Rick, a talented architect with classic style sensibility and a level head. A calm disposition was needed, as this would be a huge undertaking. In fact, this would go down in Pub history as the all-time most stressful business project.

As General George S. Patton once said, "Pressure makes diamonds." It is no exaggeration to say that the Belgian Bar of today is a Hope Diamond of the beer world and a crown jewel reason as to its top national ranking. If you think it was easy to bring into being, then you've been drinking too much Lagavulin 16-year-old single malt scotch.

Dave's high enthusiasm and crystal clear vision were soothing to Mike and Tom throughout the project. His brilliant eye for detail had always made him a dream client for builders and designers. "Dave knows what he wants and can execute it without much fuss," says Volkmar. True, that is if you don't put a sledgehammer in his hands.

Imagine for a second that you are a skilled mason, standing in front of a seventy-five-year-old brick wall. You've been hired to perform delicate brick surgery on said wall for the sake of safety and monastic posterity. As you carefully ponder how to best make the transition from this facade through the next, your client—a monkey of a bar owner—suddenly picks up a sledgehammer and starts banging away. As the historic brick starts to crumble before your eyes, your client grins like a schoolboy and says, "See, we're great at hammering walls," (see Part Two, Everybody Stepped on a Nail).

Mason Philip Raines was horrified and shouted, "No, NO!" as he grabbed the tool from Dave Blanchard's hands. As he surveyed the damage, Philip felt relieved that the minor indentation did not land in the path of his proposed plan: a triple archway fitting of an abbey. The guys would turn Dave's boo-boo into a cool candle ledge. The mason wholly understood Dave's aim, which was to give the Belgian

Bar a timeless feel, as if it had always been there. He would need every original brick possible *intact*.

After he created the wall opening (with enormous wet saw blades) and secured the structure, Philip reverently cleaned all the bricks and re-cemented them to the outer arch surface. Here came next the trickiest element of the entire expansion, matching the mortar to the original cement chips. Philip nailed the color exactly, a feat as satisfying as if he had brewed a perfect Trappist Westmalle Dubbel himself.

Belgian Dubbel (Westmalle Dubbel): A rich and malty beer with some spicy, mild alcoholic characteristics. Not as much fruitiness as the Belgian strong dark ale, but some dark fruit aromas and flavors may be present. It has mild hop bitterness with no lingering hop flavors. It may show traits of a steely caramel flavor from the use of crystal malt or dark candy sugar. Look for a medium to full body with an expressive carbonation. Traditionally a Trappist ale, many brew similar "Abbey Dubbels" to try and emulate the originals.

Once the opening was made between the two restaurants, construction continued according the architect blueprints. The plan included a long rectangular bar on the immediate right of the entrance. Turn to the left, and you would sit or stand at a wrap-around drink rail (a wooden beam just large enough for a dinner plate). In the back left corner would be a high triangular table against an exposed brick wall. The center of the space would pose a challenge as the Sweet Melissa's kitchen oven vents were shooting straight up and through the roof. The plan was to enclose the oven vents and create a square bar island with a drink rail and stools. Finally, five tables would sit in the small alcove to the left. It was time to get busy.

Volkmar and his assistant Rahím (dubbed "H & H Construction" for the Hobbit and the Hippie) took out the finished ceiling and left the low rafters exposed. In the process of removing ceiling joists, a beauty of a skylight was found in the alcove. These joists yielded gorgeous 100-plus year old heart pine wood then used for the drink rails. The unattractive, non-medieval sheetrock was hideous, so Volkmar suggested wood paneling to cover it up. When that option turned out to be cost prohibitive, the boys took matters into their own hands to find a solution. They combed the Lakewood antique market for treasure and scored rows of old doors—including one from a morgue, tiny cabinets included—that looked stupendous on the walls.

Wherever possible, the bar was constructed in old world spirit, down to the use of traditional cut nails used to hammer the heart pine floors. Although it turned into quite the ordeal, the guys sanded and distressed the floors themselves to make it look old and rustic. Lucky Tom was the only owner on hand the day the lumber got delivered. He got to lug the entire load up the stairs himself into the non-air conditioned room. Tom became an instant fan of Chimay White ale that day, courtesy of the August heat and humidity. It's a wonder the bar got finished at all, considering there was a high gravity beer tasting every day at five o'clock. Hey, someone had to taste those samples. High gravity beer was never sipped finer than while sitting on sheetrock buckets in the hot southern afternoon.

Beer heaven—a chalice of St. Bernardus in the Belgian Bar

The bar's quirkiness continued to develop. When they finally hid the Sweet Melissa's oven vents, the seating structure blocked the room's chi on the one hand and created breathtaking intimacy on the other. The beer taps, inspired by a North Carolina restaurant, were made from cast-iron plumbing apparatus. Although squeaky clean, the taps were so rustic-looking that they made some observers do a slight double-take.

The space filled in nicely with stained glass, red leather half-mooned shaped booths, and Trappist-only décor (including a 1950s interchangeable Flemish safety poster, molded Rochefort bottles, and a Westvleteren beer box available only through case purchase at the Abbey of Saint Sixtus). A rectangular, textured concrete bar with wood inlay and rows of hanging glasses put a real Italian maraschino cherry on top and *viola*! The Belgian Bar was transformed from an old storage spot into a European transporter that landed you in an old world of truth, elegance, and distinction. "I like it to be apparent that thought has been given to every detail, no matter where you look," says Dave.

The Belgian Bar is stunning, however if its beauty only ran skin-deep, the Brick Store would never have been in the running as a world class beer bar. What's most important is how well the fermented liquid runs out of those cast-iron beer taps. It takes supreme skill to properly handle Belgian kegs, a competency the Pub staff has raised to a sophisticated art. To better explain the incredible delicacy of these products, here's testimony from Matthias Neidhart, native Belgian, assiduous fine beer devotee, and owner of B. United International, a specialty beer supplier with a distinctive portfolio of world classics:

> *Dave is so fantastic at Brick Store Pub. He is at the cutting edge, pushing the issue. That's what this business is all about, excitement. It's not at all about the marketing gimmicks. We want to offer incredibly complex liquids; we don't care about packaging and labeling. And Dave feels the same way. He pairs it so well with his kitchen.*
>
> *When we are doing business across thirty-six states, in every market there are one to three players that push the envelope. That's what Brick Store Pub is in the state of Georgia. This is the guy and the place. Others are following his lead. That's what Dave has been doing ever since I met him. Incredibly knowledgeable, he travels a lot and has a mindset of going after the most complex and exciting brands. The beers look absolutely gorgeous with the glass. The windows of the Pub are very reminiscent of a small Belgian pub.*
>
> *Dave is taking on some of our beers on tap that are*

extremely difficult to pour due to the level of carbonation. He jumps right into it. He does not shy away. He is the total opposite of others. When rare beers come in (with huge explanations) that they are very difficult to pour, we can only service accounts that are capable. Dave is ALWAYS the first to sign up—"I'll take 12, 16, 20 kegs." Across the US many people know him. He enjoys a great reputation. He is in that top tier.

Dave stimulates whatever is happening in Georgia. We try to give him as many kegs as possible. He's unbelievable with his level of risk. Sometimes we disappoint because we cannot give him what he wants. For example, De Glazentoren from Belgium, their top brand is Sassion d'repe-mere. Twenty kegs came into the US; Dave wanted twelve and he got two.

Continually Whet the Appetite: Newly Arrived, Beer Dinners, Cheese Pairings

The Brick Store is dynamic—constantly evolving. Brewers love to experiment in their vats and the Pub boys love tasting the latest and greatest offerings. If it's outstanding, then that beer gets put on rotation. Thus, nobody behind the bar waits to break out the good china—every day is a special occasion for their guests. Leaving no question about freshness, a huge rectangular chalkboard hangs in the upper right corner of the bar proudly announcing "Newly Arrived" in bottle and draught. The drink menu changes twice a month, so if you want that new beer or instantly love it, you had better order it right now because it might be gone tomorrow.

That's not to say we don't celebrate big at this fine drinking establishment. A "Ten Years Ten Kegs" countdown was instituted for the Pub's tenth anniversary featuring the wildest, most obscure beer available at that time. The place was jammed ten days running as the Decatur community gathered to witness the nightly tapping of a new and glorious handcrafted keg. It was great fun to see what came out of the tap next.

Well, some of these offerings were downright strange, truth be told (that's what happens when your brewing geek fans want to send you their weirdest stuff). For instance, the following year's event "Eleven

Days of Kegs" saw a small, bluish-green barrel arrive on the bar that looked like a movie prop from *20,000 Leagues Under the Sea*. The wood appeared mildewed and the metal castings were a bit rusty. Did this keg travel to Decatur via submarine? Once tapped, brown liquid splooged out of it and tasted just as expected. Beer geek faithfuls swallowed with pride and pretended they were merchant marines. A few days later the exact opposite landed on the bar—a stylish, classy, pristine keg of JW Lees Vintage Harvest Ale with B. United International burned onto its top. The gleaming wood was a beautiful warm brown rimmed with red paint around the top, evoking the richness of England from which it hailed. Beer geek faithfuls swallowed reverently and pretended they were toasting with Princess Diana. Both kegs now sit atop the main bar.

Long time patrons were lucky to have a smooth wooden bar seat on the last night of the tenth anniversary bash. That night the culmination brew was a Scottish keg of Harviestoun Lime and Ginger Bitter (a fruit and vegetable beer style). If that flavor wasn't quite to your liking, you were certain to be offered something else delightful. For instance, owner Mike Gallagher stopped by a number of tables, his arm extended with a magnum bottle of Stone Brewing Double Bastard. With a jovial smile Mike encouraged his guests to take a sip of this full bodied, rich, strong, syrupy ale.

It was a special party and well deserved for the humble proprietors who never tire of wowing their patrons. While the guys acknowledge that their business came along just as the craft beer industry wave began a major break, the truth is they could have kept on the shoreline and watched the action from dry land. Instead, Dave, Mike, and Tom continually rose with the tide and went against the current of boring bar culture. A prime example of this was a new maneuver introduced in the Pub kitchen after almost a decade of pumping out casual pub fare: beer dinners.

"I may never be able to drink all the Brick Store beers, but I will try."

—Marie Halevy

Whereas the regular Brick Store menu is orchestrated for speed and consistency, beer dinners are a slow, ever changing, multi-course feast, where each part of the meal is paired with a different beer. Served elegantly in the Belgian Bar, these dinners are arranged with one single honored guest in mind: Mother Nature. More complex than wine, beer is a grain-based beverage as versatile and diverse as the Earth's bounty. With its enormous range of flavors and aromas (even textures), beer can be paired harmoniously with anything. Complement it, contrast it, accentuate it, seasonally celebrate it, just don't be late for the Pub's beer dinners. Word to your Mother.

Author Stephen Beaumont broke new ground in his 1994 book *A Taste for Beer* when he captured the notion of beer and food parings and encouraged us to imbibe with the rhythm of the seasons. "There's a reason we like to drink a crisp pilsner in the hot summertime and curl up in front of a winter fire with a nice scotch ale or Barleywine," Stephen explains. He refers to the popular "localvore" movement made up of people who only eat foods that are locally grown and produced. It follows in the same vein that certain beers are also best consumed seasonally (even locally) with the peak harvest time of their ingredients like delicious fall pumpkin ale (see below).

"After rejoicing at the top of Stone Mountain in autumn's crisp, blustery air, my partner Anne and I rode our bikes to the Brick Store to celebrate my favorite season with a Dogfish Head Punkin' Ale. It was a perfect drink completing a perfect fall day." –Mark Erba, Pub regular

Pumpkin Ale (Dogfish Head Punkin' Ale): Often released as a fall seasonal, pumpkin ales are quite varied. Some brewers opt to add hand-cut pumpkins and drop them in the mash, while others use pumpkin puree or flavoring. These beers also tend to be spiced with pumpkin pie spices, like ground ginger, nutmeg, cloves, cinnamon, and allspice. Pumpkin ales are typically mild, with little to no bitterness, a malty backbone, with some spice often taking the lead. Many will contain a starchy, slightly thick-ish, mouth feel too. The best versions use real pumpkin, while roasting the pumpkin can also add tremendous depth of character for even better results, although both methods are time-consuming and tend to drive brew masters insane.

Before he started writing about beer, Stephen knew he had to learn how to taste food properly. "When I was growing up, the North American experience of eating food was total detachment from its taste. Kids thought it was really cool to eat a TV dinner off a metal plate in tiny compartments. We were not programmed to taste our food," he relates. Whereas people were hungering for wine knowledge in the '70s, today there's an intense desire to know about beer. "Beer is where wine was twenty years ago," the author states.

It's a trend that delights the Brick Store boys who were all too happy to grow in their own appreciation for pairing food and beer. By the ninth year of their business, Dave, Mike, and Tom became enthralled with notion of offering beer dinners. They approached this new phase like kids running out the front door to play at twilight and nabbed a fresh playmate along the way, chef Eric Ottensmeyer. Eric could not resist the invitation to lead the Brick Store's next level of gustatory games and gladly joined the payroll.

Beer dinner "meetings" took the tone of fantasy world rather than board discussion. For instance, on a Tuesday morning in the Belgian Bar, golden sunlight is sifting through the skylight. Dave, Mike, Tom, and Eric are slouched in a red leather booth planning the Unibroue beer dinner menu. Easy discussion revolves around the bounty of spring season and the different options for making dessert reductions. The table is completely littered with the Unibroue beer: a 12-ounce bottle of Trois Pistoles, a draught of Eau Benite, a corked 750 milliliters of Chambly Noire.

"What? Our meetings are always like this," quips Tom with a sip. Jokes get swapped back and forth in total guy-culture fashion as they read labels and laugh over each other: "Blending beer with champagne. Naaaaw! That's total BS. You can't get two-in-one-shampoo." Some might say you can't get two-in-one (savvy and silly) in business professional, but we at the Pub know otherwise.

Unibroue Beer Dinner April 3, 2007
Reception:
Yellowfin-Avocado Wontons, Sesame and Soy Pork
Ephemere
First:
Seared Sea Scallops, Jicama-Daikon Radish Slaw, Pear
Nectar
La Fin Du Mon
Second:
Slow Braised Beef Short Rib, Roasted Garlic Polenta Cake,
Trois Pistole-Tomato Jus
Trois Pistoles
Cheese:
Goat Cheese Sorbet, Pistacchio, Australian Sea Salt
Chambly Noire
Dessert:
Belgian Kiosk Waffle, Quelque Chose Syrup, Espresso
Whipped Cream
Quelque Chose

The guys stayed on the cutting edge of their potential and soon journeyed into an ingenious domain explored by less than a handful of colleagues in metro Atlanta: beer and cheese pairings. Because they share the same two bacteria and yeast strains, beer and cheese are on the microscopic level "a chemical marriage made in heaven," explains local beer expert Jessica Moss. No biology degree is required to understand the splendor of the pairing, evidenced by the loyal following on every first Monday of the month. Patrons literally sob if they overlook the Pub's email notice. Wouldn't you too? Who wants to miss the magic of slipping into the softly-lit Belgian Bar lair on a weekday night, stuffing your face with beer, bread, and cheeses of the sharp, soft, blue, red, and herb-encrusted varieties (and so many others)?

Mike Gallagher sure doesn't, describing his low-key event as "delicious and fun" without a drop of pretention or technical talk (unless asked). "We're not high brow," says Mike who loves the excitement of his guests and the learning opportunity for his staff. "Around fifty people come up. It's a Monday. They dig it and we dig it." Enough said.

Bob Townsend, editor of *Southern Brew News* and longstanding Pub enthusiast, was a loud voice for cheese plates at the Brick Store. Growing up on a farm, Bob remained forever wistful for the taste of fresh dairy and intimately understood the power of fragrant garden tomatoes. "I lobbied a long time for cheese pairings. I'm glad to see they finally instituted it," he says with a session pint of Wells Bombardier in his hand. An intelligent and devoted beer explorer, Bob once brought a stash of good chocolate to the bar and invented pairing of his own (no one he shared with complained).

Meanwhile downstairs, the Brick Store kept beer nerds coming back for more with semi-regular cask ale tastings, a true brew lover's treat and a favored pick in English pubs. The rarity of a cask ale night provides a gathering point for passionate beer discussion similar to a limited wine tasting. Served out of a wooden vessel called a firkin, cask ale is unfiltered, naturally carbonated (it has no CO_2 lines), and very delicate. You never know what the firkin will spill out, so be careful. Firkins get cranky if they are not laid carefully on their side and vented the night before. It gets even messier if daddy barkeep rocks the firkin cradle too hard when he's hammering in the tavern handle. The yeast gets all shaken up and not even a firkin genie will help—you'll just have to wait a spell before that fussy baby is poured. In short, "Casks are a pain in the rear end and featured by less than one percent of Georgia bars," according to Terrapin Brewery lead brewer Spike Buckowski with love in his voice for both his cask bundles of joy and Uncle Brick Store's dedication.

At the Pub, unusual is the usual. Take the Uerige Altbier, an offering that's only brewed twice a year, which is perhaps one of the most sought-after altbiers in existence. Indigenous to Germany's Rhineland, atlbier is an ancient style of ale that predates the region's well known lager brewing method. These full-bodied babies are abundantly consumed and best produced in the state capital of Düsseldorf. As for the rest of Germany and indeed the entire world, this is a high demand beverage and almost "mission impossible" to find by the bottle in the United States. In Georgia? Well, we don't mean to brag, but at this storytelling juncture it is indeed a fact that the Uerige Altbier can be found on draught rotation at the Brick Store main downstairs bar (classic alt, sticke, and dopplesticke). It's just delightful to see it suavely sipped in traditional, petite 0.2-liter glasses, particularly by Volkmar, the Pub's German translator, who gave this reaction to tap atlbier in Decatur: "Whaaaat? Who got this here? I had trouble finding this when I was back home!"

Altbier (Uerige): A Düsseldorf specialty, this is a German style brown ale, top fermented, traditionally conditioned for longer than normal periods of time. "Alt" literally translates to "old" in German and derives from the Latin word "altus," which means "high" (referring to its rising yeast). Extended conditioning mellows out its fruitiness and produces an exceptionally smooth, delicate brew. The color ranges from amber to dark brown. It is medium in carbonation with a great balance between malt and hops. "Sticke" is a stronger altbier version, thus a bit more malty and hoppy.

It's no question that a cutting edge beer bar is going to offer rare beers. While this is exciting for the customer, it's also a high for proprietors whose fervor pushes them to get those beers through the doors. Passionate importers act with the same ardor, such as Merchant du Vin (MdV), a significant player in the Brick Store's success. MdV's zeal for fine beer collection drove them to pursue the import rights for the very limited reserve of Rochefort Brewery products, including Rochefort 10, a highly respected Trappist quadrupel (rated the number one best beer on planet earth according to *BeerAdvocate*, December 2008) and a Brick Store darling.

Rochefort beer is made at the esteemed Abbey of Notre-Dame de Saint-Rémy, where for many decades the monks had worked carefully to resell their beverages to the public through Belgian sales agents. However, the astronomical demand and finite supply pushed the monastery to desire a greater knowledge of the path their Rochefort was making from the brewery to the consumer. In faith, they granted the prized licensing agreement to MdV, as the small importer was already handling two other Trappist breweries, Westmalle and Orval. This fact considerably increased the abbots' comfort level, or as MdV's Georgia sales representative Rob Nelson put it, "They decided to dance with the ones that brought them."

This accomplishment was worthy of a big celebration, so MdV planned a grand kickoff in just two United States locations. Just as you can imagine that monks do not do keg stands out in their courtyards, you can rest assured that a company like MdV focuses on the finer point of beer such as education, history, and ingredients (versus lifestyle promotions like "Belgium Spring Break Fiesta"). MdV was clear that the Rochefort event was to be held in a real beer bar. Their final selections were the famous and venerable Monk's Café ("Belgian soul in the heart of Philadelphia") and the Brick Store Pub in Decatur, Georgia.

As party plans got underway, every single regional rep wanted the shindig in his area. However fortune smiled on Decatur as the company president had made a recent pass through the Belgian Bar. The big chief easily gathered the Pub's authenticity with its educated staff, proper beer storing, and correct stemware. He and Rob got the wheels in motion that night and flipped the idea to MdV marketing manager Craig Hartinger. Craig didn't have to scratch his head for long, as he too had been watching the beer explosion in Georgia with the ABV law change. Besides, Athens was home to national beer judge and beer columnist Owen Ogletree's annual Classic City Beer Fest. Georgia always had a great beer culture, so why not?

On June 22, 2005, beer industry folks poured into the second floor of the Brick Store Pub for a beer gala. In attendance was no less than the chief counsel of the Belgian trade commission and his assistant, the Belgian chamber of commerce representative, and the layman responsible for the Trappist beer itself, Rochefort head brewer Gumer Santos. Beer writers and editors were scattered everywhere—Bob Townsend from *Southern Brew News*, Daniel Bradford, Julie Johnson and Keith Klemp from *All About Beer Magazine*, *World of Beer* blogger and beer author Stephen Beaumont, and the Alström brothers (Jason and Todd) from *BeerAdvocate Magazine*.

It was a very special event with tons of bar owners, a PowerPoint presentation by the brewer, a delicious food pairing, an open bar of Rochefort 10 and 8, and a great buzz. "It was awesome," remembers Dave Blanchard. "My wife had to pour me into the car," laughed Rob

Nelson. He was more than pleased at the reaction of MdV's head honchos, who spoke in glowing terms of the Brick Store's best foot forward, "They were a complete pleasure to work with and the party was perfectly done." Perhaps he'd had too many Rochefort 10s, but even MdV's Belgian exporter rep Alfonse got emotional and "went nuts" over the Belgian Bar's treatment of the products and the kitchen's perfect pairing. *Aaaaaahhhh.* Sweet.

Dave feels grateful for this event, as it helped put the Brick Store on the map as a distinctive beer bar. For his bartenders it was a delightful celebration of their deeply loved Rochefort 10. "They couldn't keep up with our demand for it," remembers former Pub manager Anna Jolliffe. Although never a beer dork, Anna was always recommending Rochefort 10. "We were so enthusiastic of this beer. I worked the night of the party and we could feel the mutual appreciation of the brewers and distributors. It was a complete embrace between the beer and the bar."

They are simply crazy about good beer at the Brick Store. Not only is it the place where beer industry folks congregate, it also is the bar where sales reps bring other accounts to taste tap samples (and thus help close their deal). As local beer professionals will attest, the Pub's high gravity enthusiasm spread through the local area (some say the state) and influenced other establishments to "draught" off the craft mania. Nick Kirbabas, a former broker for North Coast Brewing Company, sums up this whetting of the appetite with a resounding hallelujah:

> [In the past] *we have serviced the Brick Store with twenty kegs a month of Brother Thelonious abbey ale. That is a "crapload" of beer. It's unheard of. They're probably one of the biggest accounts in the country.*
>
> *People are looking for unique and different beers. They pulled Bass because Budweiser now owns it. Stella and Bass are still great beers, but the Brick Store would rather carry something like Oskar Blues or Lagunitas rather than something you can get in every grocery store or every tap. We're noticing a lot of retailers, even some larger chains, see what the Brick Store is doing and they now want to offer more of these Belgian beers.*

As an industry professional, it makes me feel like what we're doing is sinking in, coming to fruition. Our message resonates here. We rely on distributors for our beer education, but most don't have the time. You'll find a hundred wine and cheese tastings, and only a handful are pairing beer and cheese or doing beer dinners. There are a lot of things out there that need to be discovered beyond American domestics. Decatur is a hotbed of people who appreciate good beer.

Be Present

It happens all the time. A guest will ask the manager, "Who is that tall man running about, who looks like a server but clearly is not?" "Why, that's one of the owners," manager Kelley Turner genuinely replies to a shocked pair of ears. Many people cannot believe that in this day and age the head honcho of a successful place would be carrying plates. Welcome to the true magic of the Brick Store Pub: simply being present.

More than any other reason, the presence of the loving owners is the sticky glue that binds the elements of the Pub into a cohesive whole. The key word here is "love," rather than distrust, workaholic, micro-manager, or a host of other low-vibration distinctions usually associated with the "boss man." Instead of averting gazes or hushed tones when the guys are coming down the hall, a cook might actually jump out and hug one of his employers in a burst of silliness. He'll get a manly hug right back, as these three proud papas boldly display their love for their employees.

It's the little things that go a long way with how the staff and the owners relate, like sharing your new pair of shoes with your boss. "Look, Mike, I got new Dockers!" a server gushes while showing off her feet. "You sure did," Mike replies in a tone that makes you feel like he's talking to his sister or a niece. When possible, the owners go to their bartender's rock band show because they simply like the people they hire. It's no wonder then that being around is pleasure by design.

The Three Amigos

"I get to show my staff that it's cool to hang out here all day and still have fun. It's not just a job, it's what you do," says Tom Moore of his Monday through Friday Pub presence. Consistency, pride, and a light heart send a clear message to his kitchen crew, who keep great attitudes despite sweltering, cramped conditions and the inevitable rough shifts. It's not utopia mind you. It's a restaurant family with all the quirks, mood swings, and normal realities of human relationships. The difference between this and other workplace "families" is that here Dad is generally around to soothe the scrapes and he truly enjoys his children.

"I consider myself a server," says Mike Gallagher with heartfelt humility. Here is a man who could be a statesman lapping up the cream of his prosperity, yet he's in the trenches with his managers on a balls-to-the-walls Friday night, arms loaded with dirty dishes and a wash towel. At the Pub's very first beer dinner night featuring selections from Unibroue, Mike is all-hands-on to lug the elegant dinner plates up the Belgian bar back steps. "Somebody forgot to tell these guys that they are successful business owners," comments the company representative with noticeable awe for the guys' hustle.

Business as *un*-usual comes easy to Mike who is awake to the fact that it is the servers—not the owners or even the bartenders—who wait on 80 percent of his customers. Being present on the floor in a friendly manner allows him the grace of understanding both sides of the booth and bar. He exudes a true desire to help his staff, not to judge or watch them behind their backs. If a management issue pops up, Mike bridges it immediately with his staff instead of allowing weeks to lapse. Plus, how wonderful those intangible moments are for guests when the owner himself delivers a drink to their table. "*Oh my, was that really he?*"

Have you ever felt goose bumps when peeking into an artist's studio? With passion's presence, the space veritably glows like a firefly. This is the invisible affects of heart and soul pouring forth into form. Pulling back the creaky door handle of the Brick Store evokes a similar experience. "My job is a hobby, and how cool is that," says Dave Blanchard with a spot-on explanation of love at the Pub. No one is more appreciative than he is regarding the Pub's uber-cool beer bar status, loving the fact that there really is only one Brick Store for beer in metro Atlanta.

Where many restaurateurs forget the little touches once their doors are open for business, Dave expands his aesthetic vision on a daily basis. Much like a craft brewer hunched protectively over a vat of barley and hops, Dave remains vigilant over the minute details of the Pub, whether it's moving one of the numerous coat hooks a few inches or pruning a creeping ivy vine. Striving for betterment and beauty at every turn, he affectionately showers his 3,500-square foot brick baby with loving attention and it shows. "Hey, nice touch," someone calls to the craftsman as she observes Dave's latest gift to the Pub: a single tuft of moss placed in the crevices of that old wooden door.

Again, the Brick Store's national top tier bar ranking transcends the actual beer menu. Rather, it starts deep in the well of caring about every single thing that makes the Pub tick. This includes maintenance practices, such as Dave changing light bulbs twice a week. Being twenty feet high on a wobbly ladder deepens his clarity that "it takes constant dedication to make it right." An hour later, Jeri, the day bartender, wanders up the stairs searching for the exact right Belgian tripel for her customer. Jeri receives quick expert advice straight from the source and transfers Dave's love from cooler to clientele. This man stays alert to his space because that's what it takes to make the Pub the best it can be.

Like many others, Dave lives by this credo: if you want to be cutting edge, then give it your all. His enthusiasm for life is reflected back perfectly in the story of Brick Store bartender Miles Macquarrie's first place victory in the 2008 Atlanta regional Guinness Perfect Pour contest. If you're new to the famed black stout, simply know that Irish Guinness is rich in history and steeped in lore, which includes serving a pint of it under very particular and exacting conditions (that is, if you are worth your salt as a bartender).

Miles' big win stood on the shoulders of a long Guinness infatuation at the Pub. The fever ran so high among the first year staff that a special beer drink was made duly named the "Shannonball" for staff darling Shannon Barnes. But then the love affair waned a bit. Once upon a time Volkmar royally pissed off the bartenders by refusing his pint. A native German and stickler for protocol, Volkmar found shortcomings in the Pub's temperature conditions which made for inferior Guinness. He told Dave plainly that, sorry, but he had begun to seek out Twain's for a superior pull from bartender Paul.

This became a challenge for Dave who began to nearly mock his friend's patronage, "Why don't you go down to Twain's, we hear their Guinness is better than ours." The beer visionary just couldn't stand that Volkmar was right, so he improved the environment of his Guinness by moving it off the long draw (the long keg lines that ran to the cooler in the back of the restaurant) and into its own little keg box right behind the bar. With this finicky Irish black beauty safely secured, the Pub could now ensure more control over the velvety beer's setting.

Fast forward years later to the day of the regional contest. Prodded on by Dave Blanchard's characteristic urgency, Miles and two other Brick Store bartenders, Bryan and Cozmo, took on the challenge of pouring Guinness perfection. At the time, it wasn't clearly stated in the rules as to how many representatives were allowed per bar. Dave planned on taking every liberty by registering a barkeep from Brick Store, the "Belgian Bar," even borrowing a spot from Twain's as they weren't sending one of their own.

It was an overboard move as anyone off the street could enter the contest. However, the mere notion raised the Pub's internal excitement considerably. Volkmar even received an urgent call from Dave insisting that he get to the Pub as fast as possible so he could judge his bartenders' practice rounds. This was a logical move as Volkmar was responsible for fine tuning the Guinness experience at the Pub. He also was well versed in the passion of Miles as a bartender, particularly when pouring the Irish stout. "I'd often watch him stand to the side to examine the building of his Guinness," states Volkmar.

Volkmar arrived at the Pub to find three frenzied men pouring pint after pint of Guinness. It became an all day affair that saw the crew storming down to Twain's to continue their pouring drills. Bryan and Cozmo seemed to channel Ireland as they consistently built beautiful black glasses that grew perfect menisciuses above the rim. In contrast, every single practice attempt of Miles' dripped disappointingly (meaning the beer head went down the sides of the curvy pint glass). As his technique continued to fall short, Miles began to sweat as much as his glass.

See, the fastidious young bartender had entered the same contest the year before and was disqualified in the first round for taking things too lightly. Not only did Miles go out early in front of his entire Decatur bar community (the contest was held at the local James Joyce), but then he was painfully ribbed on a daily basis for the next six months. The 2008 contest was all about redemption. His Pub brothers understood this and agreed that Miles was to be the main Brick Store representative.

The starting time grew near and the five men raced out the door and across Midtown to the contest. Participants looked for their names on the bracket board to see when they would compete. The judges included no less than the Ireland Guinness brew master himself as well as the first North American bartender ever to spill the legendary black beer into a glass (hey, no pressure). Looking sharply for six factors— exact glass condition, pouring tilt, tap faucet placement, a three-quarter first pour, arching dome-effect second pour, and head quality—these officials advanced only the best bartenders to the final bracket round.

Bryan faded fast, while Cozmo won some rounds and found himself going head to head with (and losing to) his coworker Miles. Vexed, Cozmo was clear that his friend's redemption train was headed to one place—the top of that perfect Guinness. In an extraordinary show, Miles let all his bad practice pours fall away as he hyper focused. His cascading pints remained consistent and he advanced to the finals.

When the judges declared the winner, *Miles Macquarrie*, the young man's eyes welled with relief and gratitude as he embraced Cozmo with a word of manly appreciation, "Brother." As Dave watched with a giant papa's grin, Miles proudly accepted the first place cash prize and brought glory home to the Pub. Well done, son!

Belgium Beer Brewer Bike Tour (or Bust)

Let's properly wrap up your education on the craftsmanship of the Brick Store with a couple stories about the Belgian Bar and Michael Gallagher's gift for bringing world craft beer and people together harmoniously.

A man by the name of Henry Wischusen reluctantly became a kitchen home brewer thanks to the persistent cajoling of a good friend. After paging through a recipe book, Henry decided to make a Chimay Red style. His friend arrived with the necessary pots, hops, and malt and four weeks later, they sampled the result. Not only was it the best beer Henry had ever tasted, it was the very first beer his wife Penny had ever enjoyed. The couple became instant Belgian beer lovers. Thanks to Georgia's new ABV beer law, their trips to the beer store became adventures in search of exotic Belgian ales. As Henry continued to brew clones of Belgian ales such as Gulden Draak, Saison Dupont, Rodenbach Grand Cru, Double Enghein, Barbar Honey, and batch after batch of Chimay Red, Penny continued to "assist" her husband as chief kitchen sampler.

About a year later, the couple road tripped to Florida with good friends and Brick Store regulars Brian and Suzie Purcell. It wasn't even an hour into the trip when Henry and Brian discovered their mutual interest in home brewing and a strong preference for complex Belgian beer flavors. For the next 400 miles, the men traded war stories, brewing tips, and hunting grounds for great Belgian beers. That is when Henry and Penny learned of the Brick Store Pub and the well kept secret of the Belgian Bar.

Both couples agreed to rendezvous at the Pub on the first Monday after their return. After fighting their way through the evening traffic, Henry and Penny found themselves happily seated on those smooth wooden bar seats and more than ready to sample delicious, authentic Belgian ale. Michael

"A fine beer may be judged with only one sip, but it's better to be thoroughly sure."

—Czech Proverb

recognized Brian as a regular and greeted the group warmly. The proprietor was excited to learn of the home brewers' mutual passion and of the Wischusen's "virgin" experience at his establishment. For the next several hours, the couple pinched themselves as they took one delicious sip after another of the actual beers Henry had copied, as well as many other Belgian beers they did not know existed.

Before the friends left, Michael presented an unlabeled bottle explaining that this particular beer could not be purchased outside of Belgium, describing it as one of the highest rated beers in the world. It was his last bottle from a trip to Belgium and Michael offered to share it with his first-timers and dear regulars. "It was a Westvleteren! So fantastic and beautifully balanced," says Henry. "We were honored and privileged to share a toast." Through that sip, the newest Brick Store "emissaries" understood that a true Belgian ale experience must include a Trappist pilgrimage.

A year later, after a fifty-mile cycling trip in north Georgia, Henry and Penny sat around with their friends drinking cold beer and musing life's greatest question, "What could be better than this moment right now?" The answer came immediately: if they were in Belgium drinking Belgian beer after riding a long ride over the famous routes of the great Belgian road races. Six months later, the couple had sold sixteen Flemish-minded adventurers on a glorified pub crawl of Flanders.

A compulsory trip to the Abbey at Saint Sixtus was in the plan, but no one could anticipate how difficult the Trappist beer run would be. On a first attempt, the group came within six kilometers of the Abbey but became saddled by strong headwinds (and a side trip across the French border for a ten A.M. glass of red wine) and had to turn back for lack of daylight. Two days later they made another 50 kilometer one-way bike ride to the town of Westvleterlen and thankfully the walls of St. Sixtus came into view. The Belgian ale lovers peddled down a narrow street lined with cedar trees and arrived at the monks' doors. Shuffling into the visitor's center, they ate cheese sandwiches, drank heaven in a glass, and crammed their allowance of one six-pack each into backpacks. Henry's lopsided bag almost toppled him near the train station as he was also managing a pack of Abbey glasses and a decent buzz from quaffing three or four high gravity beers. The Georgia shepherds wrapped their fragile gifts in their dirty clothes and made it back to Decatur without a scratch. It was a sweet victory to present the esteemed Westvleteren bottle to Michael.

It's been proven that if you can't go straight to the source of pure Trappist pleasure, the Belgian Bar makes for a mighty fine consolation. Here's testimony from Pub fan Pastor David Slagle of Veritas Church:

> *My best friend Michael and his wife Jenni have four small children and were long overdue for a vacation. As Michael's family hails from Belgium, they made big plans to visit there. A series of mishaps forced them to cancel their trip and as you would expect, they were sorely disappointed. My wife and I decided to take action. We arranged for a babysitter and took them out to the next best place—the Belgian Bar at the Brick Store Pub. All night we enjoyed great company, great food, and Belgian beer. Mike, one of the owners, came to our table and heard the sad story of a canceled trip to Belgium. As usual he talked to us at great length like we were the only people in the place. It was a beautiful night.*

Part 2

Conversation

"You are the most blessed person on earth if you find what you love to do, and do it with people you love to do it with; for people you love to do for, and if those people want you do to it for them!"
—Mark Sandlin, graphic designer and ten-year Brick Store regular

"I tried Internet dating for a while. About every other person lists the Brick Store as their favorite hangout.
—Emory University undergrad

When you are in the Brick Store Pub, you are treated like a guest in the house. In this house, that means a getting a casual, warm welcome from a relaxed person who gladly fetches you a drink—and one for your dog. There are no cookie cutter servers or overbearing managers executing business plans here. Rather the Pub runs on a family approach. Just don't ask to move in or sleep over, as that's reserved for an inner circle and happens only on special occasions.

The pulse of Decatur can be found inside the four brick walls of the Pub. Cool, in an intelligent way that steers clear from being trendy, the Brick Store Pub gives you something real to talk about: beer, bands, kids, fundraisers, civics, politics, architecture, scientific research proposals, organic farms, entrepreneurial endeavors, and artistry of every stripe. Just about everyone is into something and comes to the Pub ready to share (like troubadour Kodac Harrison stretching his first painting canvas). It's adult show-and-tell, where creative expression and everyday interaction are safe and encouraged. On the flip side, if your day, week, or year has felt like the pits, there's no need to pretend. Just come as you are, no dress code required, and be yourself—whoever that is in the moment.

The Theory of the Third Place

Have you ever noticed a gathering of two or more fathers in the hardware store aisles on Saturday, as if they had planned it? Dad's announcement to the family, "I'm going to run some errands," goes way beyond the realm of dutiful provider. Rather it reveals an inner need to flock with birds of a feather different than the wife and kids. A man's family brings him joy, and along side of that is a pile of responsibility that revolves mainly around the dinner table and office water cooler. Sometimes Dad wants a break (same for Mom).

In the structure of most daily lives, home and work are priorities, as they should be. A nagging itch develops, however, when we feel contained in a two-dimensional lifestyle. We want to scratch the itch of our human potential. So when the stir-crazies of home (the first place) and the confinement of work (the second place) threaten our emotional sanity, we head for communal rejuvenation where everyone knows our name: the third place.

"The third place" is the informal heart of a community, according to sociologist Ray Oldenburg, Ph.D., who coined the term in his book *The Great Good Place: Cafes, Coffee Shops, Community Centers, Beauty Parlors, General Stores, Bars and Hangouts and How They Get You Through the Day* (Paragon Books, 1989). Oldenburg asserts that a critical importance of the third place is to provide vital social lubrication for neighbors who otherwise might pass each other in the grocery aisle like anonymous ships in the night. Thus, spaces such as pubs, beer gardens, coffee houses, and barbershops become reliable havens that softly tie community bonds. Even a street corner can serve as a third place if people stop and fall into casual togetherness with regular passers-by.

So what has us breaking at an intersection to converse with an acquaintance? It's the burning yearning to know ourselves more completely and to be immersed in the joy of human connection. How wonderful it is to walk away from a conversation, however brief, with something greater than we did before. It might be a smile, an answer, a hot lead, a comforting touch, a belly laugh, an insight, an invitation, an inspired thought, a reminder, or an entirely new perspective. The possibilities are infinite.

A barren social circle with no third place is like a bicycle wheel with only two or three spokes. Not only does that bike function poorly, it sits lonely in the garage with nowhere to put those decorative streamers for the Main Street parade. In contrast, a vibrant third place, such as the Pub, holds the space for ten, twenty, thirty spokes,

> *"A bar is better than a newspaper for public discussion."*
>
> —Jim Parker, on the importance of a healthy pub culture

and more, its wheels gleaming with bright colors and veritably shouting, "Come on over here and let's go for a ride!" In Decatur's case, it's "Let's go to the Pub for a pint and some fish and chips!"

Maintaining happy, healthy first and second places can demand boatloads of personal energy. As nourishing as these two worlds are (best-case scenario), the third place satisfies a substantial craving to develop ourselves through lighter avenues. The beauty of a third place is how it allows us to hit life's reset button with relative ease. We enjoy a richly satisfying stretch of time while expending a fraction of the emotional calories we do elsewhere.

This isn't to say that our third-place conversations are all fluff. Oldenburg makes the case that good great places foster democracy and invite social change. Partly because of their relaxed and open nature, third places hold natural space for weighty discussions typified by tolerance. Who wants to fight about politics, religion, or culture in the warmth of the community gathering center? Reading editorials or blogging on websites are fine activities, but they will never reach the "live essay" effect that comes from one-on-one discussion with someone whose opinions or lifestyle is different from ours. There's no book report either, and the topics are varying and ongoing. Like the sewing circles of our matriarchal ancestry, our third place conversations are picked up like patchwork quilt and put down at leisure, as we thread our talking needle with pleasant grace and the yarn of our choosing.

Oldenburg's suggests that the hallmarks of a true "third place" include: inexpensive or free goods and services, food and drinks, high accessibility, close proximity to other local businesses, habitual congregation of regulars, a welcoming and inviting atmosphere, and the opportunity to see new friends and old. Hmmm. These points clearly match the Brick Store vibe. Perhaps the scholar's research was conducted under the influence of a Belgian Bar cheese plate and Dupont Saison? This is a reasonable joke, as over 400 Internet reviews of the Pub sing the same song of gladness: easy, breezy, inexpensive, inviting, non-intimidating, engaging, train accessible, and pedestrian friendly. In one customer's summation, "The Brick Store is a no-brainer."

> **Saison/Farmhouse Ale** (Dupont): A sturdy, very complex style, which is traditionally brewed in winter to be consumed through the summer months. After almost becoming an endangered species, it is now experiencing a massive revival, especially in the U.S. Many farmhouse ales are very fruity in aroma and flavor. Look for their earthy yeast tones, and mild to moderate tartness. It has lots of spice and medium bitterness. It tends to be semi-dry with a touch of sweetness.

Women's feelings about the Brick Store solidify its reputation as a welcoming place, specifically a place with a genuine sense of safety and security. This is a five-star attribute in any gal's personal guidebook, particularly with regards to a bar. Females bestow glowing praise on the Pub that it is "the polar opposite of a vapid pickup joint, a place where I can eat and drink in peace and not get hit on." Not only is this refreshing and miraculous, it also points to a timely shift in overall consciousness about how men and women can relate to each other. Hey guys, take note. Relaxed conversation not leading to anything works great with women, too. When that old, boring tension of unsolicited male advances is removed, a world of possibility opens up. You might just find a friend.

Realtors love the Pub, too. Many a couple freely admits that they bought a home right off the Square based *solely* on its close proximity to the Brick Store. One such wife laughs at her husband's thinly veiled "secret plot" to move the family from Nashville to a home within walking distance of their favorite neighborhood spot. Her suspicions were confirmed at the closing table when the presiding lawyer asked the couple, "Hey, didn't I see you at the Pub last night?" Turns out the real estate professional had been sitting just a few feet away. Coincidence? No, as her husband spilled the beans while signing his life away. Numerous business trips to Atlanta had included many visits to the Pub, thus the family's Decatur move. Today they are proud city residents and elated parents who enjoy leisurely walkabouts to the Brick Store with their child. In the kitchen hangs their display of love at the Pub: local artist James Dean's rendition of the Brick Store. That sketching is also printed on the first page of the Pub menu. Coincidence?

James Dean, creator of popular art figure Pete the Cat, elaborates:

> *The Brick Store is a magical place. The owners had a great vision and found this little building and saw what it could be. They created a simple place for people to come and talk and drink some beer. I love SIMPLE, it's what I try to keep in my artwork. Every painting I've ever done of the Brick Store sold well. I started asking why and found out how much it means to people.*

Pete the Cat at the Brick Store Pub

We Are Family: Diversity at the Pub

Thriving diversity at the Brick Store deserves special mention. Since opening day, the non-pretentious Pub has been a neighborhood magnet for people from all walks of life. It has created its own unique culture, so highly regarded that it might well be emblazoned on a "third place" welcome mat. The pull of this avant-garde bar scene has spread to metro Atlanta and brings in just about everyone who is sick of ordinary, patronizing, loud, crass drinking establishments. As long as you are well mannered, you can stay.

Look around the horseshoe bar stools on any given day and you'll find a blue-collar worker sitting next to a corporate lawyer, who sits next to a gay couple and their child, who sits next to a pastor, who sits next to a beer geek, who sits next to a tattooed carpenter, who sits next to a fifth-grade math teacher, who sits next to a local bluegrass guitarist, who sits next to a philosophy professor, who sits next to a punk rocker, who sits next to a visiting grandfather and his grandson. You can be fairly certain that they have asked about each other's pints and occupations, perhaps even sampling them or trading contact information, respectively.

The community absolutely loves that everyone comes in the Pub and gets along. It warms the soul to witness people from different generations, lifestyles, and educational levels engaging authentically with one another. It makes no difference if conversations between the suit-and-tie and the poetry book are short-lived or even a tad one-sided. What counts is the unspoken willingness shared by all that we are here to be free, be sociable, and be immersed in an amazing beer culture. We let go the stringency of social norms, at least until our pints are empty and we're out the door. Call it a reality coat check.

A great example came on an ordinary weekday night somewhere after eleven P.M. when Gene Clerkin, D.C., founder of the Center for Holistic Health, sat down at the bar. The Decatur-based chiropractor leaned over an empty bar stool to extend a greeting to another patron who he'd recognized from an earlier visit, local carpenter Craig Rafuse. "Are you in the same stool from when I saw you last?" Gene quipped with Craig as the two men, in their late-thirties and mid-fifties respectively, fell into easy talk about their delicious beers and the glory of the warm evening.

As the pair swapped chitchat about the architecture of the Pub, Craig grabbed the horseshoe bar with both hands to make his point tangible. He then pointed to a barstool where a woman had shared her incredible story of being an innocent young bystander who got swept into the mayhem of the 1968 Democratic Convention riots. As if on cue, another man a few barstools down moved closer to make it a three-way conversation. Tony, a remote biologist and former Army employee, had a few teenage adventures of his own, namely drinking and singing with CIA officers in a Beirut café at the tender age of eighteen.

"These are the kinds of conversations you have here," Craig emphasizes of his new friend's tale. Tony chimes in that he's lived in thirty different locations (currently the coast of St. Marys) yet there are so few places like the Pub that he can step into and immediately feel at home. "It's like walking around someplace in the 1950s where you always know someone." Gene adds that Decatur itself is unique, a constant feeling of *eureka!* For him, the most beautiful aspect of the no-nonsense Pub is striking up agenda-less exchanges, which, even if occasionally contentious, allow him to get a better rounded picture of life. "If you're interested enough to explore different conversations and drink these fantastic beers, you may even leave the country one day," Gene winks. A lull comes as the three men sip their beers in unison. Dr. Gene reads their minds: "We're confident about the beer here."

Although Craig is usually absorbed in a good book or editing his own writing (a project on the history of *The Wizard of Oz*), the carpenter is always willing to peek his head up from his barstool and join the crowd. Craig feels the Pub's vibrancy as a growing and knowing place, loving that his conversations enhance both his life and the life of his community. Craig continues that he can speak to people of all ages at the Pub and relate to the "youngsters" with his musical tastes of the Rolling Stones and Mothers of Invention, a fact lost on his twenty-four year old nephew (who thinks his uncle is lame). "I don't get that reaction here," says the regular.

On the flip side, there are enough Brick Store "geezers" so Craig can check in and affirm this stage of life. It's a nice sight to see retired couples strolling Decatur's walkable streetscapes, many of whom like to step into the Pub for early evening fellowship. One such pair is Charles and Laura Molton, who have lived a half mile from the Square for over three decades. Married in their early twenties, Charles and Laura met through fascinating circumstances in 1966 when Charles dialed into a telephone recording nicknamed the "sputnik line" that had a vague reputation as a "place to meet girls."

Back then, old fashioned telephones had heavy receivers and a dial tone that went *CH-CH-CH-CH-CH* when you dialed the number. There was no such thing as an answering machine, however this bizarre sputnik line served as a very strange chat room for metro Atlantans. Basically, if you called a phone number that was inactive, you were put through to a recording that tied in all unused numbers in the area. This telephone dead end then became an open line where you could hear other people. If you get your hands on one of those phone numbers, you could call and shout over the recording, "Are there any *girls* on the line? My name is Charles Molton, can I ask you out on a date?"

A Decatur High graduate, Charles got himself invited to a party through the random sputnik recording and spotted Laura strolling across the neighboring yard. He marched right up to the love of his life, walked her home, and that was it. They got married a few years later and rode out the changing decades when Decatur was an unpopular place to live. Thirty years later, the couple strolls up to the Brick Store to sit at the bar, hold hands, drink beer, and talk with their neighbors young and old. "This place is an anchor. We love it. We know the staff, we love the guys and they seem like they take a lot of care in making it good." The sixty-something-year-old lovebirds also appreciate the continually new offerings from the horseshoe bar. Relegated to American style mass-produced beer, Laura didn't drink much before she discovered the Pub in 1997. Now a European ale fan, the Loganville native started her beer career off properly—with a Guinness.

Another gal who baptized herself with suds under the warm, dim lights of the Brick Store was Amy Laurent, Agnes Scott College senior, who had her first legal pint at the stroke of midnight on her twenty-first birthday. Her hot date? Beloved Mom and Dad. Her pint of passage? A Samuel Smith's Organic Cider, which sat on the sturdy wooden table and stared at Amy for a full ten minutes before the clock turned twelve (as time had made her wait this long, she wished to be taunted by it for just a wee bit longer). Her parents gently chuckled as the young lass swished her "sweet elixir" in its tall glass and thumped her head in self-inflicted agony on the table five minutes before the witching hour.

Amy felt the friendliness of the cider pint drain with each painful minute, wishing for the red model airplane slanting ominously above her head to come crashing down. At 11:58, she began to feel the heaviness of the bar chandelier and imagined the faux wood vines encircling the indoor lampposts to be barbed wire. "Time had put me into maximum security," the young lady dramatically bewailed. Amy steadied herself by assuming an adult vibe and decided that the late Thursday night crowd and the Pub were "poised to honor me, as my lips met alcohol."

At a minute before the hour, her parents toasted their daughter's life thus far and wished her many more years to come.

Midnight on December 5, 2008 at the Brick Store Pub. The Religious Studies major brought the glass of organic apple cider to her lips and daintily set it down after taking just one sip. Amy's journal captures the moment of the milestone: "The taste quenches a thirst imposed by time. Satiated by that dribble of fluid, I sink into my seat and yawn. I'm not thirsty any more. Not tonight, at least."

Amusingly, Amy's father had discovered the Brick Store before she did while he was "doing the dad check up thing" of her college life. On subsequent trips, he'd take Amy to dinner and then send her home early to the dorm so he could explore the Pub's drink list and make friends at his "new favorite place."

While it's quite typical for parents to introduce their offspring to the Brick Store, it's a wind that blows pleasant back where young adults call their mom to "come meet me at the Pub for a brew!" The Johnsons—Lynn and Wayne, and sons Craig, Darren, and Colin—are another one of those local families who raised their children around Brick Store whiskey barrel tables, watching them grow from teenagers into young men.

As each son took a turn to celebrate his twenty-first year around the horseshoe bar, the magical transition was made where Mom became "friend" and Belgian Bar buddy. Always stopping at the Pub after their golf games, the brothers nurtured a warm relationship with the staff, playing in bands with some and dressing as the bartenders for the annual Halloween party. Lynn treasures her closeness with her boys. They treasure her too and their friendship with their mother extends to their friends that has extended to her favorite Pub nickname, "Mama J" (dubbed by a son's friend). Colin just smiles at his friends' awkwardness when Mama J shows up to knock a few back, as he knows that the Pub "is even ground and no one's turf." Besides, he taught Mama J how to golf, so where else is she supposed to go? With the close-knit vibe, charismatic staff, and best beer in town, the Pub is almost as good as Colin's own living room. Now that's a "family meeting" we like to hear about.

To put a finishing stripe on the family flag, here's a quick visit with Kelli and Kelly, a young couple who each discovered the Brick Store on her own. "I always feel welcome. I always feel good," says

Kelly of her Pub visits, "and it's not because I've tipped back three gravity beers." Describing herself as a "pure cider girl" before the Brick Store defined her appreciation for beer, Kelly is enamored with the staff and the restaurant's policy that every server is your server. As a former waitress, she feels strongly that the management would not hire someone who didn't know how to take care of you (even if she and her girlfriend might get a little loud while sipping Belgian ales under Decatur moonlight). As Kelly emphasizes her extreme comfort level in the Brick Store, Kelli pops out a story: "This older lady came up to us, gushing that 'Oh, I've had a few beers and I just want to tell you that y'all are so cute. You remind me of my daughter. You are very cool, I bet your moms are so proud.'"

No TVs to Infinity

A sense of belonging and feeling understood are universal needs. These vitally precious gifts are developed, among other ways, through shared times and rich conversation. But how do we break through to a soulful exchange, those talks we never want to see end, the ones that nudge our hearts and open our minds, and lead us to a space of self-reflection? How do we get to a full belly laugh with our friends, which have us bear-hugging each other goodbye at our cars? How do we get to "hello" with a stranger and thus swing open a door of opportunity? It starts with the basics: active listening in conducive environments (read: no television sets).

Brick Store Pub is a bar industry leader for many reasons, however it could be argued that the decision to nix the boob tube was their crowning achievement. This policy ultimately nourished and fostered everything else for which the owners took a stand. World-class beer deserves attention and discussion, as do the authentic surroundings in which you are drinking it. A warm, inviting atmosphere is seriously compromised if you cannot focus on your companions. Courage to strike up a conversation with someone new is nearly impossible to muster when your barstool buddy is absorbed in the hypnotizing glow of an electronic box.

Savvy folks bring out-of-towners to the Brick Store because they know it's the go-to place for real social intercourse with family and friends. Without the competition of background noise, they can dote on their craft beers and loved ones. No surprise, their guests have a lovely time and ask to come back on every visit. That's because they've shared fond memories, swapped stories, discussed important life events, and, according to some, "Planned strategies for taking over the world." Even if an interaction lasts only a few minutes, it's usually genuine at the Pub, so you turn away feeling satisfied, like you would pushing away your finished turkey burger plate.

Call it emotional intelligence, call it common sense. TV is simply unnecessary in any fine establishment. Love at the Pub isn't about numbing out with mindless distractions, it's about tuning-in to and waking up to what's real and special: your company and your beverage. Can you imagine someone telling you they love you for the first time with the annoying backdrop of flashing commercials? Thankfully, Caleb Sturges had the full attention of his girlfriend Marci when he first professed his love while sitting at the Pub's downstairs bar. "We had gone to the Brick Store on many dates, and here he said 'I love you,' right out of the blue. I replied 'What?' just so he would say it again," recalls the now Mrs. Sturges.

Now, of course, every modern invention enjoys its rightful place. Television programming can create strong bonding and it certainly produces plenty to talk about. But didn't you walk into the Pub for a live newscast? Or at least to raise your vibration while listening to cool music and the sounds of laughter? Wouldn't you like to meet a new friend? Then put down the remote and go drink a pint with your neighbors!

Televisions have never been missed in this conversational pub. A patron opinion survey reveals emphatic agreement with the policy. Answers ranged from "fantastic" to "No TVs to infinity" to "don't ever change" to this gem "It makes the Pub about people." Pub cook Bill McJenkin further illustrates patrons' feelings:

Dancing Late at Night: Athens, Georgia

How'd we get such a cool place in Decatur? It's not like the Brick Store Pub dropped out of the clear blue sky. Its vision and good energy were founded brick by brick on the camaraderie and spirit of the owners who poured love, determination, and happiness into the woodwork. The back-story of their history has been told in snippets across the bar for years. Now let's hear the whole story.

This tale begins circa 1993 and 65 miles down the road due East on US Highway 78 (with a slight wiggle to the right off GA Loop 10). Follow that route and in about an hour and fifteen minutes you'll land smack dab on West Broad Street, the bustling main road that joins downtown Athens and the gorgeous antebellum North Campus of the University of Georgia. The quaint college scene back then was similar to what it is today: students and professors streaming out of class and under the famed UGA arches, and then pouring across the street into the lively business community replete with bars, shops, and plenty of restaurants.

It was here, directly across from North Campus in a converted Wendy's, where our three adventurers met as cooks, waiters, and "door guys" at the (now defunct) Mellow Mushroom, aka the 'Shroom. A popular, psychedelic-themed pizza chain, the 'Shroom was dark, narrow, neon-lit, and busy with hungry party-going students. People jammed in there for three things: a unique pizza crust, yummy Peppercorn dressing, and the enormous beer selection. With thirty-three tap brews and over a hundred bottled beers, this place gave the opportunity for better beer discovery. Even if most of the southern college football crowd stuck with domestic "swill."

The 'Shroom provided a breeding ground for friendship. It was also a place to expand your beer knowledge. Classics like Samuel Smith Oatmeal Stout, Paulaner Hefe Weizen, and Fullers ESB may not grace the Brick Store now due to their wide availability, but back in the day this was considered drinking from the Holy Grail cup. As described in the Introduction, what left an even bigger and more favorable impression on these three friends was their time spent in a beautiful Athens drinking establishment known as The Globe.

Young and fresh out of their graduation hats from the University of Georgia, where they never crossed paths, Tom Moore and Dave Blanchard were the first pair to meet at the 'Shroom. Tom had already made his way to manager while Dave started humbly as "the door guy" checking student IDs and stamping hands. The pair hit it off quickly as friends and did the male bonding thing through volleyball games. There wasn't time for much else, as Tom walked out of the 'Shroom within three months of Dave's arrival. He was sick of the penny-pinching, micromanaging attitude of the owner, which bothered him so much that Tom stormed out in the middle of his shift. Dave applauded his friend, but continued making his own way to management.

Dave's work environment became a blast as a brand new crew joined the 'Shroom staff. He settled into his Athens life and made it all about having fun in the fast-paced restaurant: playing darts and Frisbee golf, listening to local music like the Woggles, occasionally floating down the Broad River in an inner tube, and, of course, drinking good beer at The Globe. Just as the scene began to feel stale and Dave considered a change, a guy by the name of Michael Gallagher applied for a job.

Dave immediately liked Mike, an energetic, charismatic Irish workhorse from Philly, who was "fun as crap" on the pizza parlor floor. Mike seemed to have jets on his shoes, as he commanded the six-table front section of the 'Shroom. The Gallagher one-liners at the computer register made his coworkers die with laughter. First, he teasingly beat you out of your turn to type in a customer order, and then he'd zoom off with two pitchers of beer in one hand and a large pizza in the other. Dave purposefully staffed Mike on his management shifts, as much for entertainment as assuredness of getting the job done. Over and over they worked on full-to-capacity weekend shifts in this college town.

From 1994 to 1995, Dave, Mike, and the 'Shroom gang enjoyed Athens life to the hilt. They partook in lots of three A.M. North Campus Frisbee golf, late night music shows at the 40 Watt Club, occasional dance parties, and weekly brunch pilgrimages to The Grit, a favorite vegetarian place in the "townie" neighborhood of Normaltown where Dave lived. Everything and everyone was within biking distance, and thank goodness. Many times, one or all of the crew became car-less. Despite the slight inconvenience, this added a lovely feeling of innocence and intimacy to the group. The 'Shroom staff Christmas party went down in history in 1995, as an entire poster board of incriminating pictures made its way into the office (as testimony to this era, many of those same photos hung in the Brick Store office for over a decade).

Ah, the life of youth in their early-to-mid-twenties. Adventure trips to Atlanta for Music Midtown and the Six Flags Amusement Park bonded Dave, Mike, and their friends, several of whom would later come to work for them at the Pub. Dave even concocted a "Tuesday night pals" weekly dinner party where he further displayed his talent for, ahem, rallying people around his ideas. As he roped a "pal" into his scheme, the unsuspecting friend would naturally fall in line with the plan, "Oh, I'm coming to your place, Dave, and I'm cooking for you and the pals? And bringing my pot and pans? Sounds great! I'll be there." Dave would smile a Machiavellian smile and kiss the "pal" on the top of the head. No one could resist him and no one wanted to anyway.

As an aside, Tom and Mike did not meet during this time period, at least if you ask Mr. Moore. He swears he randomly met Gallagher on a trip back to Athens years later at Mike's downtown apartment. Mike, on the other hand, clearly remembers waiting on his future partner one night at the 'Shroom. Now working as a kitchen manager in the local Outback Steakhouse, Tom came back to visit his old haunt. In a polite yet punkish manner, Tom made himself right at home by stepping behind the bar, changing the TV satellite channel, and special ordering his meal in shorthand code reserved for employees. Although Mike's eyebrows arched quizzically at his customer's comfort level, the waiter just smiled at Tom's liberties. What counted is that his guest remained gracious and tipped Mike very well.

Heading Down the Atlanta Highway: Athens to Atlanta

As golden as early 1995 proved to be, Dave really had one foot out the door of Athens right before Mike started working at the 'Shroom. It was hard to leave yet harder to stay. Dave packed up his scant belongings that summer and said goodbye to his playmates and idyllic lifestyle. With little clue of what he was going to do with his life, Dave hightailed it down the Atlanta Highway to join the fledgling Marthasville Brewing Company as a beer representative. Thus, the Chamblee, Georgia, native found himself living in the Virginia Highlands neighborhood of Atlanta and scouting out restaurants and package stores within his work territory.

Life for Dave was exciting again in a fresh feeling way, as he and Marthasville proved a great match. His clients immediately fell in love with the Martha's Pale Ale as well as the tall, smiling man offering it to them. For about a year things were great. Dave explored the metro Atlanta area and pondered life in rush hour traffic (a completely new thing). Then a familiar bug of "it's time" bit him and Dave pushed for an answer to his life's purpose.

The UGA graduate knew at least this much: He loved beer, he liked working in restaurants, he easily handled the pace of a bar, he didn't mind working hard, and he knew hands-down that he could design a better place than the 'Shroom. With a hatchback full of Marthasville Sweet Georgia Brown Ale, he set out to find Tom.

Dave didn't have to look far. Tom was already there and running another Outback kitchen. Glad to reconnect, they picked right back up on their one and only conversation in Athens regarding opening their own place. Momentum fizzled again, however, as both men were consumed with their new Atlanta gigs. Notwithstanding the poor timing, the idea stuck.

Competitive in nature, Tom always knew he would be a business owner one day. It could be as a restaurateur or a pet store proprietor, as long as the establishment was his. Tom started bussing tables at age thirteen for his mom who was a bartender and fell back into restaurant work during college "for gas and insurance money." Tom quickly moved to being head honcho wherever he worked, whether as headwaiter, floor manager, or kitchen manager. Fast and focused, Tom discovered the pains of being forced to cut corners in the back of the house at Outback. Admittedly he placed high expectations on himself, even coming in two hours early for the kitchen shift so he could be completely prepared. Despite his best efforts, Tom found it nearly impossible to deliver on his personal gold standards in the stressed-out environment of a corporate restaurant chain. As job dissatisfaction grew within him, Tom renewed the conversation in earnest of opening up a bar with Dave.

They became roommates. During the middle of the Super Bowl, Tom packed Dave out of his rental dwellings and moved him into his basement apartment on the eastern border of Piedmont Park. The living room couch became their planning bunker. Placing their dream on the map included serious talks of locating the bar in small, college-friendly towns like Ashville, North Carolina, or Charlottesville, Virginia. A daring move out West even made its way into the consideration talks. Still, the guys were twenty-seven, inexperienced, and overall broke, so it comes as no surprise that they felt nervous about committing. Although dialogue stuttered and stalled, the intention remained clear: We are doing this, no matter what.

It was summer 1996 and the much-anticipated Centennial Olympic Games loomed on Atlanta's horizon. The guys were frustrated with their present work situations and antsy for change. One early morning, the other shoe dropped. Dave waltzed into Tom's bedroom and sat on his feet. Dave then started cracking his pal's toes and said, "Wake up. Go quit your job so we can open our bar." With implicit trust in his future partner, Tom got out of bed and gave one month's notice to Outback that very night. Dave gave two weeks' notice at Marthasville on the same day, and the wheels of action started turning.

"Eighty percent of success is just showing up."

—Woody Allen

Dave and Tom set themselves up with management positions at The Mill, the first and only restaurant on the grounds of Piedmont Park. A two-year plan came forth wherein the boys would save money by selling their cars and walking everywhere, including to their new jobs. As all of Atlanta was buzzing about "how much money could be made during the Olympics," surely, they figured, this upstart restaurant in the Park would provide them a big payout. Right before they started, Dave developed a foreboding and aborted The Mill strategy. In classic Blanchard fashion, he sold Tom on a smile with Plan B: Decatur.

Lucky Town: Decatur Is the Place

Lucky's Irish Bar was constructed on Decatur Square almost overnight by one of the owners of Jocks N Jills Sports Bar. Fueled by the contingency of Irish Olympians staying in the old courthouse, Lucky's opened *presto* in the building adjacent to the alley of present day Brick Store Pub. The promise of a huge Decatur Olympic Festival drew in the two energetic bucks, Dave and Tom, who got themselves hired to bartend. Bartend they did, thirty-one nights in a row on twelve-hour shifts, non-stop balls-to-the-walls. It was frenzied bliss.

Although the Festival proved a colossal flop, Lucky's was a gold mine for Tom and Dave. Netting a small fortune in this four-and-a-half week stint, they made the call *not* to get other jobs and instead put a solid plan in action. More than a month went by, a time period in which they decided to take six cases of canned Heineken and truck it down to Destin, Florida, to get some rest and regroup. Right before that beach trip, Dave made another important call, a phone call to his old Athens pal and favorite Irish workhorse, Mr. Michael Gallagher.

Dave and Mike, like Dave and Tom, had flirted with the idea of opening a bar together, however the energy of their potential partnership dissipated when Davey left town. When he got the call from Blanchard, Mike sat square on the fence about marrying the restaurant industry. He still felt happy about his Athens living situation, but was a bit sick of his job. Although Mike's dad had offered him a place in his business, an office setting just didn't feel right. Like his pair of future partners, Mike had figured out what he *didn't* want to do, namely sit in a corporate cubicle. Loosely understanding that the pair had quit their jobs, Mike listened carefully as Dave related a serious commitment conversation and an invitation to join him and Tom at the beach.

Mike hopped in his car and went to meet them, remaining in a neutral space about the whole thing. That is until he saw the proposed bar location, the very promising City of Decatur. Mike became smitten, like Dave and Tom, who'd had their eyes opened wide by their Lucky's experience. Decatur's potential was screaming to them. It was the perfect spot and talks of other locations were called off. Cramming into Mike's small Integra, the threesome drove to the beach with fluttering hearts. Mike returned to his management shifts after the weekend and left the other two car-less. It didn't matter much, as the visionaries were too absorbed in calling everyone they knew who might be able to tell them how to open a restaurant.

While Dave and Tom ate Gulf Coast crab legs and reached out for help, Mike drove thoughtfully home to Athens. As he stopped to pump gas into his car, suddenly the light bulb went on. Mike became clear on what was in front of him: the opportunity to set his own destiny. Only twenty-four years old, Mike felt scared about owning anything this big. Yet, like Dave, he felt confident that he could do much better at running a bar than his present employer. As long as he could wake up in the morning excited about the day and go to bed happy about what he had done, well, that was all that mattered to him. Even if this business failed, it was worth it to him to go for it. With the threat of a walkout looming, Mike quit the 'Shroom and made a beeline to Decatur.

It was the twilight of summer and the three partners fanned out as barkeeps, baristas, and waiters to keep their funds afloat. Only half-joking, the guys credit the Pub's initial success to their well-known employment in about a tenth of the city's eating establishments. This included Dave and Mike working at Twain's Billiards and Tap, and Tom managing the restaurant that had replaced Lucky's, The Purple Cactus. Dave also ran Church Street Coffee and played Scrabble with his girlfriend Talia Wurtzel during down times (which was most of the day prior to Decatur's renaissance). Caffeine soon became a dear friend, as the guys zoomed in on identifying their space: the De'Lite's Hair Salon right across the alley from Lucky's.

"Hey, We Built That Ourselves": Build-out

Over the course of the thirty-one long days and nights of the Olympics, Dave and Tom had an abundance of time to look over every possible inch of the hair salon. The windows were boarded up and plastered, there was a shower in the back, a staircase went straight up the middle, and gold paint adorned a good deal of the interior. Dave was betting on hardwoods beneath the thick, black and white checkered tile that covered the entire floor. It needed to be completely gutted, no question. Yet it was a classic, decent-sized commercial space, affordable, and in prime in location. Between all their restaurant contacts and a slew of contractors whom they met through Dave's elder brother, architect Rick Blanchard, they decided this was the type of place to consider. In Mike's words, "It was a place we could afford; the right building at the right time in our lives." In the words of Mike's mother and father, "Good Lord, if you can turn that [building] into something, God bless you."

Next came selling themselves to the landlord, a task that required every bit of entrepreneurial muster the guys had, which wasn't much. So they paid a visit to Glen Gurevich at Sweet Melissa's and said, "Hey, we have this idea! What's up with the hair design place?" When Glen heard their boyish American dream, he immediately found it interesting. The problem was that a local pizza chain had already approached him about the location and Glen knew the management had a pocket full of cash and experience—the lack of which made two strikes against the Brick Store kids. However, the long time Decatur proprietor felt strongly that a pub could be successful. His intuition won out over the raw facts. Glenn shared that the salon's lease was up in five months and its owners likely would not renew. He told Dave, Mike, and Tom that if they could get it together, they should come on back to see him.

At the time, the trio's collective business acumen could have fit into a paper cup. All they had for collateral was Dave's baseball card collection. So it was time to go see affluent Uncle Elwood in Pennsylvania for advice and help. Dave's relative sent them to his son-in-law Bob who worked as a small loan lender at a little bank in Delaware. On a mercy mission, Cousin Bob came to see the space and meet the partners. The trip proved fruitful. Cousin Bob went away feeling confident that they had the bases covered and it was doable for them to break even because three people were sharing the workload. The lender gave his professional speech that the most recent Dun and Bradstreet report gave restaurants a 7 percent chance of succeeding and that the partners would most likely end up hating each other. "Cousin Bob, where do we sign?" was the boys' lively reply. Thus he agreed to provide Dave, Mike, and Tom with the necessary collateral they needed to secure the loan. It was off to the races, as they began the bank loan application process, requesting only a modest $120,000.

The guys sweated out hearing back from the bank right up to the very day the landlord went forward to publicly list the hair salon property. Sick of biting his nails, Tom made yet another attempt to reach the loan officer and actually got him on the line. "Oh, 125 East Court Square? Yeah, you guys are approved." Tom's stomach gurgling, he picked up the phone again to call Dave at Church Street Coffee. "Hey man, are you sitting down? We're business owners." Dave let out a shout of "Holy fudge!" and the three musketeers entered the next phase: demolition.

Everybody Stepped on a Nail

On March 5, 1997, the guys opened the doors of their future Pub and started scraping black tile, an activity they would do during the entire span of build-out. It was so sticky and hard to remove that they went through six-dozen scrapers and only got the last blessed scrap up about three hours before officially selling their first beer. Scraping the exterior brick for an entire week took second place in the "most tedious" category. It was painful to watch that work go down the drain when they decided to paint the outer building.

Dave, Mike, and Tom might have been rock solid confident on what they wanted and where they were going, but getting the Pub physically built was an entirely different matter. Too cash poor to hire a general contractor, they counted over 100 runs to Home Depot. Everybody stepped on a nail, and someone survived a nail gun incident. Carol Blanchard's slogan became "No tools in the kitchen," as it constantly looked like an over-turned adult toy box. Dave insists that most of build-out was spent hunting down hammers and screwdrivers, as no one bothered to wear a tool belt. Organized chaos ruled.

If it wasn't Mike falling off the homemade scaffolding, it was Tom falling through the second floor and into the kitchen while trying to jam a piece of way-too-big plywood into a slot with his foot. "I thought he was dead," remembers Dave of the commotion as he came running into the kitchen. Gratefully he saw the miracle of only cuts, scrapes, and a stunned look on his partner's face. They recruited Mike's brother Ryan, a "Tasmanian Devil" character, who folded nicely into their motley crew. Ryan's idea of how to take down old walls was to make tiger saw cuts and then jump through the drywall. He fit right in.

Meanwhile, the Pub doors remained open during all of build-out. The boys stopped construction and said hello to every single person who walked in. It was better than a matinee. "Everyone in town had seen us morons trying to put this thing together—a real neighborhood affair," Dave says cheerfully of their efforts. One such neighbor was John Yale, an engineer in a local Decatur firm who told them to "hurry up," as their establishment was sorely needed (his teenage daughter Sam would go to become the first female kitchen employee).

Volkmar peeked in one day with his assistant, Brian Robinson of the band McPherson Struts, and stayed to give them a sledgehammer lesson. The boys were shocked and pleased to see a huge plaster explosion with just a hard enough hit on the walls. Volkmar ended up loaning the guys most of his tools so they could sheetrock the bathrooms. In the middle of this havoc, the carpenter's dearly beloved vintage drywall knife got sacrificed to the missing tool gods. This was love indeed.

The almost-entrepreneurs remained sweaty and broke every single eighteen-hour day of build-out and survived on takeout from Sensational Subs. Many sales representatives came in during construction hawking their food and beverage wares. The guys were handed all kinds of samples, like baking pans and bottles of wine, when all they longed for was beer and food. Mike vividly remembers a week long stretch of painting with his brother Ryan until after the midnight hour. The boys were so desperately hungry at that point that they'd break into the tiny deli ham samples and gnaw them right out of the packages. Finally a kitchen slicer was bought, and the boys made a serious request to the sales reps: big, fat samples of turkey breast. Oh my! The Gallagher brothers thought they'd died and gone to turkey sandwich heaven.

It was miniature miracles like this that kept them going. Although self-admittedly "dirty and thin," the guys claim they never had so much fun in their lives. But they wondered if they had enough money to finish the job. A smidge of knowledge and a ton of guessing kept their Excel spreadsheet budget miraculously in the black. Delighted cheers erupted every time they saved a penny, as more cash on hand meant upgrading to better appliances. Stress was a given. Enthusiasm prevailed. If you want to know the secret of staying in the restaurant business for over a decade with three partners, it's this: Frisbee meetings in the parking lot. The meeting with Wholesale Wine rep Don Lattermer went down in history as the first flying disc discussion.

The benefit of having three chiefs bore out enormously during this time. With so many daunting tasks to complete, so little experience, and barely enough capital to invest in the business, the guys' camaraderie was the main thing that kept them balanced and largely unfazed. This intangible asset proved especially valuable the morning Carolina Lumber accidentally delivered a load of planks *through* the Pub's front window. Tom's blood pressure took several years to recover from this incident. Dave received comforting pats on the back after the all-day affair of running the main gas pipeline underneath the floors and into the kitchen. "It was hot and sweaty. I couldn't see. And you just knew there were rats coming up on you. To top it off, I spent the day with a handyman who was, well, an interesting bird," he says, grimacing at the thought.

As in any good relationship, each man took his turn to have a meltdown. Tom stormed off on the arduous day he dug the power line. Mike got stressed about the look of the *outside* of the alley windows. Dave averted a nervous breakdown by eating fifty hot peppers at the local Thai place, Thai One On, thereby earning his name on a plaque. This gastronomical feat came on the eighth day in row that the hired carpenter did not show up to work. Their funds were nearly gone, and there was no chance of replacing "this moron," so Dave chilled out with a beer on Twain's patio with his friend "Fat D" and left a desperate voicemail for the contractor. "Please, you have our life in your hands. We don't know what else to do." It worked. The flaky hired gun showed up the next morning and put in a full day's work.

We were dirty and thin. **Mike Gallagher takes a rest from Build-out with Decatur resident Bruce Wynn, 1997**

To further survive the madness, the trio traded off playing hooky in pairs, even if it wasn't equitable. Like when Dave and Mike went to one of the most posh restaurants in Atlanta. Tom's favorite wisecrack to his partners still goes something like this: "You two got Pano's and Paul's steak dinners, while all I got was Braves game hotdogs. Whatever."

Another advantage of having three six-foot bundles of energy was their ability to individually focus on the various, seemingly endless big projects at hand. Tom worked his connection with a high school buddy who ran a used kitchen equipment supply company. Mike drove 375 miles round trip to Albany, Georgia, in a used postal truck to buy twenty whiskey barrels at a steal. This venture produced the standout olfactory moment of build-out: opening up that truck door and getting blasted by the smell of hot bourbon, a quart of which remained in the bottom of each barrel. Too bad they couldn't sell it.

Then there was that pesky thing called a bar. Dave's baby, he worked with Rick and Volkmar to execute his dream of a gorgeous, gleaming horse-shoe shaped bar of the finest quality. Road trip plans were concocted so Dave could show Volkmar the Athens and Ashville prototype inspirations. The point became moot, however, as the guys ran out of money before fulfilling their vision. Sucking it up and moving forward, Dave settled on cheap plywood materials. Appalling as it seemed, at least the bar did curve like a horseshoe and somewhat gleam under the skylight.

Dave made peace with the plywood and scoured the gigantic Lakewood antique market for dining room tables where he scored big-time on second-hand deals. Enthrallment turned to alarm the following day when Dave went to pick up the purchases and "could not stinking remember" in which booths he'd left them. Like a frantic lost kid, he wandered the market for six hours looking high and low for his tables. A couple of blisters later, Dave limped a quiet victory home with his new furniture.

It seemed whenever the trio's energy began to dip, the neighborhood poured in to keep the momentum going. The large northern plastered wall needed some pizzazz, so Tim Ahlenius came by and gave Talia Wurtzel a faux finish paint lesson. An improvisational actor at Whole World Theater, Tim's troupe had received many donated beer kegs from Dave over the years. David Aldrich, an original Trackside Tavern owner, showed up unannounced one day with three other guys and declared, "I had a lot of people help me when I got started. I want to help you." His crew painted the ceiling, and then painted it again without a complaint, as the boys didn't care for the initial blue color. David, furthermore, refused compensation or discounted drinks. It was a class act and a very much-appreciated gesture from a colleague and a neighbor.

Dave, Mike, and Tom contracted with their Brick Store logo artist Jody McFerren to produce an outdoor wooden sign. Jody took the brand logo, a trio of whiskey barrels, and transferred it to cedar planks using oil paint. He made it a joint project with Brian Robinson. The McPherson Struts singer carved an outer portion of the sign and seared the words "Brick Store" onto the treated planks. Each artist beveled the edges of his creation and Brian hung them in a manner so Jody's piece swung through the hole of Brian's. It became a sign within a sign and a truly beautiful a piece of art.

After two months, the project was finally completed and the pair decided to surprise the boys. Thank goodness Jody lived close to the Pub—right down from Twain's—as no one had a car and that four-foot square sign was heavy. They threw a sheet over the artwork and lugged it to the Pub with the help of Jody's neighbor Trapper Ed. The troupe walked in way after ten P.M. and presented the sign to the proprietors whose jaws dropped open. They knew it was coming, but didn't think the sign would arrive in a ghostlike manner. It was an important feature, their visible announcement to the world. Dave, Mike, and Tom loved it. Thanking Jody and Brian for their quality work, they propped the sign on the edge of the bar and took pictures of it. To this day it hangs outside the Brick Store Pub. "It's the miracle sign, because it hasn't had a single wood treatment in over ten years" says Jody, today a co-owner of Our Way Café.

Moments like these soothed the stressful fact that the guys' general contracting skills sometimes leaned toward those of The Three Stooges. All that pent-up frustration eventually got vented on the southern wall during everyone's favorite part of build-out: knocking down the plaster with sledgehammers. A huge morale booster, sledgehammer therapy provided "raw progress" and a stunning visual. A divine moment was reached when the crew uncovered five alley windows, each complete with original wood, glass, and weight and ballast systems. Discovering these virgin windows on that gorgeous red brick wall felt like the building's blessing, as if it was saying, "Oh yes, I was just waiting to become the Pub. Thanks for seeing my potential and returning my glory."

The Immaculate Conception: Building the Pub Door

If the original windows they'd excavated seemed heaven sent, the birth of the Pub's wooden door was a bona fide immaculate conception. Right before the end of build-out, the Brick Store still needed a front door. Not just any door, mind you, but a brilliant door that would reflect their highest vision. Trouble was, the door committee was sidetracked along with every other Pub startup committee. When the heck were they supposed to focus on such an important decision? Like almost any baby, it came when it came.

Andy Maslanka, another local carpenter, had once asked Dave about the Pub's construction needs. "Oh, just a front door," was the reply he received. *Just* a front door? As any builder knows, a door is the only moveable piece in a house. Its engineering design needs to be solid and it is best made in a workshop to ensure that the pieces are square and the door will actually open. In the case of the Brick Store, Andy knew this door would be hanging on an old building and getting heavy use. The carpenter was also British, and his sixth sense told him that this was to be a special pub deserving of a special entryway.

It was days before the Brick Store's opening and still no door. Although Dave had spoken briefly with Andy about building this piece, scheduling was an overall joke. When the right person showed up, things got done. Andy happened to stop by the Pub at about eleven o'clock one night, and Dave pulled him inside and laid out the urgency of the situation. "We had to have it," Dave reports. He had the cedar planks his car. . .what about now? Twice before Andy had played a role as a pinch hitter for the guys—first fixing Dave's dilapidated beer truck, and then driving Mike to Albany for the whiskey barrel run—and he would do it again, right on the Pub floor.

After a brief family discussion, Dave retrieved cedar planks from his car and made up the door design on the spot with "St. Andy the Carpenter." They threw the planks down on the floor and arranged them to their liking. Dave suggested a small, diamond-shaped window near the top, so Andy dug into his collection of "funky old stuff" and produced a stained glass rose from the set of a comedy show. With a snip-snip here and a clip-clip there, the rose was set into a makeshift frame fashioned from whatever was lying around in the trash (namely an old Coca-Cola container and some papyrus). The whole process was executed in a matter of hours. That very door has hung in front of the Pub's entrance ever since. To explain the great significance of this construction, here's a carpenter's account from Volkmar:

> *Usually a door is built in a shop, a woodworking shop—with jigs, clamps, other equipment to assist you in getting a unit together—so you can hinge it on a door jamb and it will work. It's done on a big smooth table so you can control things. Not only did they not do it in a shop, they did it right on the ground with the floor as the workbench.*
>
> *Dave had bought some cross brace tools, and they clamped the planks by drilling them into the ground.*

No way in hell should you use the floor as a clamp tool. They didn't have pegs for placeholders, so they cut off a broom—someone got pissed about that broom. They were in a creative mode to get it done, so they went through Andy's wood collection. The inside handle is a branch out of his yard, and the pipe (that used to be on the outside) was lying in Andy's truck.

They just threw it down and did it—very gutsy. Andy didn't think about it. If they lost a few weeks or a month, that was money. That door's been there for over ten years. The fact that it was made in the crudest way possible and has lasted this long is a miracle. Andy is an artist, not just a carpenter. That door is a true piece of art. It should be on the front of magazines. "How we age."

The door may be the most durable piece of art in history, considering that an estimated two million hands have touched its handle since the Pub opened. Although there are constantly things to fix, the Brick Store would never trade in the door's charm for something commercial that has no need for maintenance (the staff freaked out once when a patron silenced the creak with an oil can). Love at the Pub absolutely is present in Andy's random afternoon visits after a day's work somewhere else, pilsner in one hand, and pocket tools and a smoke in the other, tinkering with his wooden child. Under his crusty English muttering, "There's always something wrong with this door," lays a quiet pride and devotion that has seeped into the door itself, casting a reverent spell upon all who enter the threshold.

A glimpse into Andy's philosophy illuminates a mysticism that's so well placed among the Belgian monk ale being served in the Pub: "There's nothing I can *beat* in Nature. She is my muse. I've learned more from Nature than I have from anything else in the last twenty years, more than from books in the library." Blessed be, indeed.

Brick Store Pub's front door with new stained glass beer diamond

Opening Day: June 27, 1997

Tools slowly disappeared out of the kitchen and the Brick Store began looking like a pub. The second-floor balcony rail stools had become the favorite spot of all concerned to take in the view and sigh, "Yes, this is it. This is cool. It's time." Then it happened. The liquor license got approved and that was that. Faxing in their signed license, the guys received their first shipment of beer on Friday, June 27, 1997. They scrambled to put away the last of the trash and dashed home at about 7:30 P.M. to clean up, leaving a handwritten note on the door: "We'll be open at 9."

At five minutes after nine, Decatur resident Lisa Gerritzen was walking along the Square and noticed that the Pub had on its lights. Stopping in curiosity, she surveyed the façade, observed the whiskey barrel tables and wooden "Brick Store" sign, and nudged her friend, "Should we see if they're serving?" Lisa pulled the door back slowly to a very loud *CREEEEEEEAK* and peeked into the dimly lit space. It was empty except for the bartender. "Hey, are you open?" she asked as an owner waved her to a bar seat. Lisa immediately spied the Newcastle tap and ordered two pints. Dave Blanchard was busy ringing up a beer for his first customer and automatically gave her the Brick Store *schpiel*: we have no neons, no TVs, and no domestics. "Well that's great," Lisa replied affably and quite content. Thus, the second and third beers were sold.

Within a half hour the house filled up with "just about everyone" including all the owners' supporters: family, friends, new neighbors, and tile scrapers—the whole gang. It was pleasant pandemonium with a few kinks, like Ryan jumping in to save the day when Booth One collapsed. There were only about three handwritten menus floating around and a father and son's chips order got lost. No one remembers what music was playing (probably The Pogues), however the only meaningful sound was that of love, as pints were raised in well wishes. Although it would be a few more weeks before the official Grand Opening with speeches made from the steps, this was a night to remember. The rest is the history you now hold in your hands.

You're Hired: First Year Staff and Beyond

Ten fresh-faced employees were ready and waiting for customers that week. Many came from the neighborhood. Cook Reese Jones lived right down the street and was as thankful that the guys "had brought really cool beer to my hometown" as he was for his new job. His classmate Rachel Adams was another Decatur High School alum whose recent trip to Paris had her missing the walking culture. Dreading her commute to a café gig in Buckhead, Rachel instead walked down to the Square to search for employment. As the Winonna Park resident wandered into the Pub, it was apparent the guys were busy with build-out. The interview was brief and went something like this: "Hey, are you hiring?" "Hey, can you paint?" "Yep." "Grab a brush, you're hired."

Rachel convinced her Café Intermezzo coworker Sally MacGregor to take the leap and join the crew of the unknown establishment. The tall, blonde architecture student had a wide smile and quiet demeanor and wasn't quite certain about working in a brand new restaurant. Tom wasn't sure about Sally either, with her scant server history. But she was just so likeable! Tom handed her a rag after the interview and she got right to cleaning. On their Brick Store visits, Sally loved showing all her friends the tables she had stained. Once she graduated and began a nine-to-five position, Sally couldn't bear to leave and stayed on part-time despite her new boss' request that she quit. Money wasn't the issue—it was that family feeling like Tom coming to jumpstart Sally's car and knowing all her regulars by their beer orders. Once she left Atlanta for the west coast, Sally says she missed her Brick Store Pub family just as much as her other friends and relatives.

"Smiling Al" also had little server experience, so she had to interview first with Dave, then again with Tom, and a third time with Mike. The Pub was so close to opening by Alyssa's last interview, that when she arrived Tom was leaning over the rail and waving to her, "You're hired, grab a rag." Her nickname stemmed from a round of side-splitting banter between Mike, Alyssa, and Melissa (Langley), another server who bore enough resemblance to her coworker that Mike was becoming tongue tied. "It's too much," he cried in his jesting tone as the pair cleaned the steps. "You're Mel and you're Al," the owner pointed and roared with the laughing authority of a dear friend. Mike added the smiling part later, as Alyssa's bright personality outshone any lack of industry skill (which she quickly gained).

Dave Daniel lived less than a mile east from the Square on Ponce de Leon. He was twenty and looking to make summer money for college. His interview for a kitchen position took place with Dave, Mike, and Tom while seated on the floor eating pizza and drinking Warsteiner. The Paideia School grad tried to act cool in the June heat as the proprietors seriously asked him this critical job skills assessment question: "So, would you rather be gored in the calf by a bull or hit in the sternum at close range by a golf ball of Tiger Woods?" Dave Daniel smiled and swallowed his pizza, as he knew where he'd be spending the summer.

Toma Oliver worked in the Brick Store kitchen for eight years including the 1997 opener. The longest job he'd ever had, the Pub worked for Toma because of good management. "I left a job where I was treated like a child and came to a place where I was treated like an adult." Toma also felt fueled by the people around him, particularly in the kitchen where every cook was in a band. He loved the constant exposure to new worlds of music, endless shop talk about instruments, and the camaraderie formed from seeing each other's bands including his own (loud rock group Something Left After Misfortune).

Year one of the Brick Store was extremely mellow for employees compared to the high volume, labor intensive environment it is today. Sometimes it was so slow in the kitchen that the staff would experiment by deep frying every food item in the house. Tom remembers back in the days when they only had one server for an entire Saturday. The first weekend slam saw poor Mel running her tootsie off with nearly every table sat in the restaurant. "Tom!" she cried to her boss, her Bettie Boop-like face all red and sweaty. "Don't freak out, Mel, just tell them they'll have to wait," the captain said while steadying his ship from the kitchen galley. The waitress sold $500 in sales that afternoon (a figure that two or even three servers can easily match and outpace on any given Saturday today).

As the Brick Store family grew in staff and patronage, so did the responsibilities. Dave, Mike, and Tom's magnetism naturally attracted team players who wanted to grow the Pub as much as they did. Long time-manager Kelley Turner and server Santi "Puma" Deshnad reflect on some of the meaningful aspects of their employment as they bask in the sunshine at the Sweet Melissa's tables, the day shift regular hangout:

Kelley: *Dave gave me the nickname "E-Y" as soon as he met me. He likes to spell everything backwards and speak in pig Latin. I came from a long restaurant background in Athens—both Mean Bean locations, Rocky's, Five Points Deli, Guaranteed. I worked corporate for two years in a medical review office. It was boring and I hated the hours. Now I can walk to work. I do the payroll, receive the deliveries, get in the bread and produce, set up the books, take care of the windowsill… plants make a subtle noticeable difference here. Whatever needs to be done. I also do the shopping at Sam's Club and get snacks for the servers like fruit yummies and chocolate chip cookies. Most places do not get snacks for their staff.*

Santi: *I've worked here for over two years and also at Squash Blossom. I came from a hotel corporate restaurant. I get so much more freedom here, it's so relaxed and I can mingle with my guests. There's no uniform and people take care of each other.*

Kelley: *Two separate couples told me today that they met here and are now getting married. Tons of couples ask to have their wedding reception here. A Georgia Tech department wanted to bring their entire graduating class. We just can't do that. I do love that there are still enough regulars that I see twice a week. Many have quit coming in as much because we're so busy all the time. There's so much more for you here in this field [for staff]. The guys are like family, you can tell them anything. When Dave's children are here, I'll help watch them.*

Santi: *When it's packed at Brick Store, sometimes customers will bring their kids down to Squash Blossom to play in the kid's room until their table is ready. One time on a slow night I brought in $60 worth of big fat steaks for everyone. The kitchen cooked those babies up good! We like to eat good here, so why not?*

Todd DiMatteo, who is seen most regularly behind the bar on day shifts, is the epitome of a laid-back Brick Store man. Although he'd lived in Atlanta on and off for nine years, Todd had never set foot in Decatur before joining the Pub roster in 2005, except for the Friday night when his fiancé finally wooed him into a Brick Store booth after endless talk about the best beer spot in metro Atlanta. As Todd absorbed the warm ambiance, over three Gonzo Imperial Porters, and the music of The Rolling Stones (*Exile on Main St.*), something clicked deep inside him. The friendly yet understated veteran bartender knew if he was going to continue in this industry, he might as well do so in the most creative environment possible. Todd asked his sweetie if it was fine to ask their server, Ryan Gallagher, for an application.

Soon enough Todd found himself seated in the dimly lit Belgian Bar waiting for his job interview with Mike. From his cozy back corner booth, he says it felt as if he was hanging out in some cool 1940's Communist hangout of Frida Kahlo's. "It felt ridiculously relaxed." Then Todd went through a "grill session" with his prospective boss, as Mike Gallagher hammered him with questions for an hour and a half. The next day Kelley followed up with a ten-minute informal meeting. Todd asked if tattoos were okay (yes), and just like that he was hired. A few years later, Todd is still found making drinks behind the day bar. That is if he's not engaged in a round of coaster toss with Dave Blanchard.

Baltic Porter (Flying Dog Gonzo Imperial Porter): Porters of the late 1700s were quite strong compared to today's standards, easily surpassing 7 percent ABV. Some brewers made a stronger, more robust version, to be shipped across the North Sea, which they dubbed a Baltic Porter. In general, the style's dark brown color covered up its cloudiness and the smoky/roasted brown malts and bitter tastes masked any brewing imperfections. The addition of stale ale also lent a pleasant acidic flavor to the style, which made it quite popular. These issues were quite important given that most breweries of the day were getting away from pub brewing and opening up breweries that could ship beer across the world.

Brick Store Tenth Year Staff Reunion

In June 2007, the Brick Store celebrated a decade of world-class beer, friendly service, and casual dining. A staff homecoming party was part and parcel of that milestone. Folks flew in from all corners of America to attend the bash, which came complete with an anniversary tee shirt, a "Welcome Home" banner, lunch buffet, and kitchen band reunions. Old coworkers came to pay homage for a minimum wage job that cashed out a mint in emotional dividends. It was a massive gesture of respect on both sides of the employee-employer fence and an amazing testimonial to the power of love at the Pub.

Of course, hardly anyone remembers the details as the party was held all day and night at the Brick Store with an open bar (incriminating digital photos showed up the next day). Soggy interview notes of mine yielded some additional information, such as the fact of Jason Embry informing his new bosses that, "Hey thanks for giving me a job. Now that I'm hired, I need ten days off because I'm getting married." Jason remembers not having enough time to laugh at Mike when the owner came running down the service hallway and jumped over a Guinness keg that the bartender was rolling to the cooler. "I wanted time to stop, it was just like [the classic video game] *Donkey Kong*." Like so many other employees, Jason also had a funny story of hugging and thanking the guys to the point of being inappropriate (a normal occurrence at Pub staff parties).

Michelle Thomason, an early Brick Store hire and former bassist for the Athens band Supervixens, didn't recall feeling relaxed while busting a move on her waitress shifts. However, the Pub became a touchstone as her life's journey continued. Among many beer trips to Decatur, she sought the Brick Store's comfort first thing upon moving back to Georgia and immediately following a horrible tragedy in her family. Michelle deeply appreciates that even though she is unfamiliar with most of the current Pub staff, she always feels welcomed and relaxed inside those four brick walls.

One of the most touching moments occurred around twilight, when an open microphone gave way to impromptu personal sharing from Pub alumni and present staff. Smiling Al said it best with simple, straightforward thoughts on her time working for Dave, Mike, and Tom. "All I remember was how much fun it was to work here. The guys would go upstairs at night to count the money while we cleaned up. And then we'd sit at Booth One and hang out until four in the morning with a scotch or a beer. Sometime's you'd talk for fifteen minutes, sometimes three hours—an overwhelming feeling of good times and good friends."

Thank you, Brick Store Pub.

Part 3

Community

"Did you say you were from Atlanta? Have you been to the Brick Store Pub? I went there for a wedding, and that is one of the best pubs I've ever been to in my life."
—An Edinburgh native and actor, commenting to a visiting Decatur couple while on their pub tour of Scotland

"My dad introduced me to it [the Pub].*"*
—Slightly embarrassed guy in his late 20s

"It's greater in Decatur" is a tune sung by many a resident as they stroll along tree-lined streets to one of the many shopping districts here in this beautiful, historic, small city. A snapshot of life in the late afternoon is a vision of teenagers on their skateboards riding home for dinner, school crossing guards smiling as they stop your car for the children, scores of folks jogging or meandering to the dog park, Agnes Scott College students walking to the library and coffeehouses, and the counter service girl from your favorite local eatery riding her bike to work. It just feels like home.

"Hey, where have you been? We missed you, girl," the Decatur meter maid calls to Chachee Valentine, a former Brick Store Pub server who has just moved back to her adopted Southern hometown from Los Angeles. After two years of barely hearing a "good morning" from her West Coast film industry coworkers, this warm, offhanded greeting blows her mind. "I knew I made the right decision in coming back," Chachee sighs in gratitude as she locks up her bike.

Cars are blessedly optional here in the City of Decatur, home to 18,000 residents and a daytime population that swells to about 24,000. Short work and school commutes via foot or bicycle are common here, as is hopping the train to Atlanta at one of three nearby MARTA (Metropolitan Atlanta Rapid Transit Authority) stops, including one that sits right under the Square. Those shared Zip cars? Yep. Come borrow the keys. Although the community shared bike program is a bit come-and-go due to transient rental space, there are tons of places to ride on two wheels, including Decatur's wide stretch of PATH trails (Georgia's nationally recognized model of recreational biking, walking, and rollerblading trails).

Let's not forget our four-legged friends and our wheeled travelers: the city boasts three dog parks and a skateboarding park. Makes it easy to see why the Decatur community knows each other so well, doesn't it? We literally travel the streets together.

If You Build It, They Will Come

There's a truism that "where attention goes, energy flows, and results show." If you want to be a great town, then you must act like a great town no matter what the present circumstances. Take the City of Decatur, a place which from '60s to mid '90s suffered commercially, as families moved to the suburbs and businesses languished. Today a trendsetting "City of Excellence" (Georgia Municipality Association, 2006), the Decatur of yesteryear was deader than a doornail. Residents' memories of those times gave the impression of tumbleweeds rolling down the street. As one native put its, "You could park a Winnebago in the cul-de-sac [Square] past five o'clock."

During this time, the city's bright personality barely shined for lack of downtown meeting places. This is not to say that brave proprietors weren't opening up shop. Landmarks like Seventeen Steps and Final Touch (opening in the '70s), Eddie's Attic, Sweet Melissa's, Terra Mater Salon, Food Business, Trackside Tavern, and Grog Shop (opening in the '80s) held down the surrounding Square area. Eateries like Twain's and Crescent Moon successfully staked their claim in the mid '90s. Still, an Atlantan's image of Decatur as a cultural or commercial destination in those years would have prompted the bemused question, "Isn't that where you go get your driver's license?"

My, how times have changed. Decatur of today tells a story of determination, innovation, and vision. A quick glance at the city's growth statistics show that restaurants more than doubled between 1996 and 2006 along with a boom in shops, galleries, and service centers spread throughout the different commerce districts (including the Square, West Ponce, East Decatur Station, and Oakhurst Village). The City of Decatur has also won a pile of awards for community involvement, city planning and design, walkability, and transportation. So while many folks give the Pub sole credit for reviving the Square, the truth is that Decatur had been putting out the Brick Store Bat Signal way before Dave Blanchard, Mike Gallagher, and Tom Moore were of legal drinking age.

Something Very Grand

To better understand the Brick Store's early success, first pull up a chair to a community-planning meeting, circa 1980, at which city stakeholders and government officials commissioned a two-year study on the Square's economic revitalization. The seventeen-member Decatur Downtown Redevelopment Task Force dove into the challenge, initiated a citizen hearing process, and produced a comprehensive forty-six page advisory proposal (for the sake of anyone whose attendance at community-planning meetings are sporadic at best, that's massively impressive). This proposal became the Decatur Town Center Plan (1982). In summary:

> *The overall goal is . . . a traditional and intimate small-town center . . . to maintain the tradition of humanity and warmth that has been Decatur's from the 1920s, the kind of small town in which people can walk downtown to shop and do business in an atmosphere of intimacy and friendliness, while at the same time providing for economic revitalization and expansion.*

With great integrity, the Task Force kept their eyes on the prize of a town renaissance that would strengthen the sense of community. These citizen meetings, glowingly described as "dynamic," drew people from all walks of Decatur life to envision the best possible work, live, and play scenarios for themselves and their families. Dreams were built upon an existing foundation of neighborly trust, pedestrian-friendly geography, an engaged school community, and memories of greatness. A notated comment in the Town Center Plan underscores this last point: "When I was a child, we used to go to The Candler for Sunday lunch [on the Square] and it seemed to us to be something very grand."

Thanks to committed Decatur stakeholders, oh how grand it still is. Cheers, y'all.

It Starts from the Top: Decatur Visionaries

In the City of Decatur, civics isn't that high school class you barely passed. It's like breathing air. Our small urban center vibrates family friendliness and "smart growth" to its core because the city government and business sector work hand and hand with the citizenry. "We ask people what they want, so our progress comes from, and is driven by the community," says Linda Harris, Assistant Director of Community and Economic Development. "Thus, you buy in to who we are. Whether you've been here for two weeks or fifty years, you are part of the community."

That's quite a warm welcome if you are a new business owner. Ask Talia Wurtzel Blanchard, co-owner of Twain's Billiards and Tap brewpub, restaurant, and pool hall, and also of Squash Blossom boutique. When she and her brother Ethan looked to open Twain's in 1996, an antiquated law sat on the books that prevented pool halls in the City of Decatur. Lyn Menne, Director of Community and Economic Development, not only worked to change the code, she also stopped off in Philadelphia while on vacation to see the pool hall owned by the Wurtzels' father, Howard. "Here they were, great young folks with an interesting concept for a family-friendly restaurant that we thought would be successful in Decatur," said Lyn. "The City Commissioners were willing to listen to the idea and agreed to make the changes necessary to allow the business to open. Twain's has been a wonderful addition."

The seat of DeKalb County, Decatur was named for U.S. naval hero Stephen Decatur and incorporated in 1823, twenty-five years before Atlanta. It's more than plausible that Decatur's notoriety would have eclipsed Atlanta's had a decision not been taken by the city's early residents to turn away plans for a major railroad stop in the 1830s. The rail line was rerouted seven miles down the road to the small settlement of Terminus, which was renamed Marthasville in 1843, and then became Atlanta two years later. Just imagine young widow Scarlett O'Hara from *Gone with the Wind* being sent to see Aunt Pittypat in Decatur for rejuvenation of her spirits. Rhett Butler absolutely would have been drinking single malt scotch and smoking a cigar at the Brick Store Pub.

Oops, we don't smoke anymore here in Decatur—ever since a city ordinance was passed on the heels of a countywide smoking ban that went into effect July 1, 2004, the same day as the Georgia beer law change. "That was an interesting day," remembers Dave. While a few still lament that they can't light up a stogie while sipping a Black Maple Hill small-batch bourbon, the no-smoking policy is overwhelmingly hailed as a blessing, just as DeKalb County public health officials knew it would be. These committed professionals held the vision of clean air and healthy worksites, and supported the County and City Commission through semi-rocky conversations with the business community. Now no one would ever think of going back to smoking indoors. In fact, parents report that it's the reason they started coming *back* to the Brick Store with their kids.

Like other typical bar owners, Dave, Mike, and Tom wondered how exactly the new health ordinance would affect the Pub. From the onset they knew that Decatur was a family town, thus they always embraced a children's policy that was welcoming without being overly accommodating (for example, the Pub has no booster seats, kid's menus, or diaper changing stations). Many a bucket seat baby carrier has graced a Pub table because parents, like other grownups, want to go to a pub where the tradition is neighborly conversation over great pints in a cozy atmosphere—not get wasted and act like a buffoon. But still, what was going to happen with this law? Would the smokers who drank above average be replaced by legions thirsting for Shirley Temples? Would it turn into Chuck E. Cheese?

Concerns quickly subsided, as several things became apparent. For starters, there's no place on Earth like the Brick Store, so smokers simply adjusted to going outside for a drag. All those years of cultivating palates and creating a distinctive atmosphere had done the intended work. The Pub's culture was about craftsmanship, conversation, and community. Not smoking. The policy also cleared the air for a higher level of fine beer appreciation, as the sensory tools of taste, smell, and sight became unclouded.

A good number of returning families turned out to be an earlier generation of patrons who had loved the Brick Store when they were single or childless and loved it even more now that they and their kids could breathe smoke-free air. For instance, Paul and Meera Garcia were loyal Pub fans "BC" (before children). "We started and ended many pub crawls here," effuses Meera. "Now we're here with Violet (age 9) and Chloe (age 7) for the children's scene at five o'clock., and boy is it crowded!"

Former regulars like the Garcias may have disappeared from the bar stools into the baby rockers, but their love for the Pub remained, as did their natural respect and gratitude for this amazing institution. They weren't about to let their darling little rascals treat it like a fast food playland. This mindfulness became a new unspoken policy. Decatur moms and dads "get it" that nighttime is for adult conversation and their children's presence is a privilege. So they shuffle into the Pub during the early evening, order fish and chips for the kids, a turkey burger and a pint for themselves, say hello to the neighbors and the staff, and then head home right around bath time. It works out perfectly.

Dad's Ice Cream

Looking back, perhaps the guys would laugh at the mere thought of the Brick Store transforming into a kid's playground (it's more like adult home base). Parents might feel hazy to remember the name of that German eisbock they had with dinner, but they could never forget that right outside the famous wooden Pub door is a vibrant town center geared for their children's pleasure. Little Shop of Stories dedicates its entire space to children's books and events while That Pottery Place beckons finger painting on plates and saucers for Grandpa. A number of boutiques and specialty shops focus solely on children, like Hoopla that offers "fun stuff for kids." Others, like Squash Blossom, dedicate small play areas for Tinkertoys and such.

The Decatur library, just steps from the Square, is a non-stop children's zone, as is the adjacent Decatur Recreation Center. Ice cream and pizza parlors bring out angelic smiles, as do the fifty-seven acres of developed park areas—most with playgrounds—that lie within the city's limits.

Although there's no swing set or sandbox right on the Square, children are able to use their imaginations quite nicely while climbing the bandstand gazebo right outside of the historic Old Courthouse. Likewise for the garden terrace tables and mist fountain *Celebration* statue that sees plenty of youngsters making a joyful noise on (and off) their structures. All of this area comprises the centerpiece of downtown Decatur, the Roy A. Blount MARTA plaza, which went through an unsightly, yet successful $4.5 million construction overhaul from

2005–2007. Its revamping produced a much improved, wider, more open, and more accessible space for "Decatur's living room" and our numerous community and special events.

There's just nothing like rolling out your wheeled cooler and picnic blankets to enjoy a May or September concert on the Square with your friends and your little babes. The sight of children romping freely everywhere is a soul-lifting experience that reminds us of what life is all about.

Artist Gary Price on his Decatur Square Celebration statue, dedicated to the service of Decatur Mayor Emerita Elizabeth Wilson (1993–1997): Imagine a world without limits, without boundaries, without prejudice and blame. Imagine an existence full of self-confidence, self-esteem, and not only tolerance, but love for others, regardless of color, socio-economic, or any other standing. To me, that is what the future holds. That is what children represent and that is the type of world I would like to help others imagine so it can come to pass. Celebration is just that, a celebration of life and aspirations.

Then there's our beloved Pub, also known as Mom and Dad's playground, which is good for their sons and daughters, too. For instance, Chris Clark was thrilled with the Brick Store's arrival for many reasons, not the least of which was the comfort zone he felt in bringing his infant son, Declan. Saturday afternoons found Declan's baby bucket perched on a steady barstool while Chris enjoyed a pint and the paper. As the years rolled on, father and son would amuse themselves during relaxed weekend lunches by drawing mustaches on advertisements in the paper and playing "I Spy" with the endless knickknacks and doodads blended into the Brick Store's background. "I spy with my little eye an accordion, a bicycle, a bumble bee."

Pub management knows Declan and scores of other kids like him who have "grown up Brick Store" from their mothers' pregnant bellies to their first days of school, and on through their high school graduations. In a few rare instances, parents have sat down at the horseshoe bar only to receive a server's "report card" on their high schooler's behavior. "Well, Mr. and Mrs. Nelson, your son Tyler came in on Saturday night on a first date and he was quite polite and tipped generously. Good job!"

"Good job," is a compliment generally bestowed to the Brick Store by many a discerning parent such as Mark Erba who, when appropriate, never hesitates to head into the Pub for a beer and to enjoy the company of his teenage son Dante. That's because Mark's philosophy as a father closely resembles that of his favorite drinking establishment: Set a good example.

Mark had seen more than enough of lackluster restaurants and gimmicky watering holes in his eighteen-year career of driving metro Atlanta's streets as a sales representative. In his mind, something was amiss if he left a bar stool feeling more unsettled than when he first sat down on it. He longed for anything close to his relaxed tavern hangouts back in Boston, somewhere he could read a book if he wanted and reconnect with himself.

So when the Brick Store opened shop, it was love at first pint. Here stood a place that stimulated his palate, mind, and soul. Here was a new paradigm in imbibing culture, an authentic pub that screamed "yes" to him from the sidewalk to the ceiling. Here was character, intention, and honesty. At that horseshoe bar, Mark felt comfortable in his skin from the moment he sat down to the time he left—a treasured sense of home away from home.

For this and many other reasons, Mark finds the Pub quite suitable for Dante. It's a safe harbor, free of ubiquitous electronic and print advertising, where a parent can connect with his teenager and be surrounded by an unpretentious crowd of adults who are focused on their conversation and the quality (not quantity) of their drinks. Mark appreciates the consistency of the service over the years, always finding his barkeeps to be adroit, friendly, and individual. It's a priority for him to be in a space where social graces rise above social dependence on a bartender or drunkenness to have a good time.

A glaring counter-example presented itself to father and son when the pair landed in the cocktail area of an eating establishment before heading to a big rock concert together. Mark's excitement about bridging the musical generation gap with his boy was tempered by Dante's exposure to excessive alcohol consumption, blaring music, and wanton body language. Not that they weren't about to see all of that at the concert, however it sent a clear message that bars were crazy pick up joints. A few months later Mark seized the opportunity to circle back to the conversation he had with Dante that night about what *not* to emulate from certain bar patrons.

It was a weekday evening and Mark had picked up his son from his lacrosse practice and headed to the Brick Store for dinner. An athlete himself, Mark had worked in a nine-mile run while his teenager ran passing drills. His cardiovascular system was still cooking by the time he reached a wooden booth so Mark ordered a Spaten Märzen, a medium-bodied, easily drinkable malty beer at 5.9 percent AVB. Dad then slid right into a talk about his beer choice, explaining to his son why he did not order a heavy stout or thick, high gravity Belgian ale. This expanded into a larger discussion on drinking appropriately and peer pressure. The Pub's backdrop of relaxed adults and families provided the perfect framework to show Dante what mature drinking integrity looks like.

On a gorgeous Sunday afternoon in springtime a different father could be found at the bar grabbing a pint before heading back to an outside table. As he scanned the drink list with his bike helmet in hand, he mentioned, "I just finished riding bikes with my daughter. She's outside with her ice cream while I get Dad's 'ice cream' from the Brick Store." His cone flavor? The sweet, malty taste of De Dolle Belgian ale.

Wise Beyond Their Years

As described in Part Two, the Brick Store owners caught a healthy glimpse of Decatur's potential during the 1996 Olympic Games, namely a burgeoning urban community with all the bones of a great city just waiting on a fresh infusion of young blood. The Decatur Business Association (DBA) had been wearing X-ray vision goggles for a long time and could see, much like Dave and Tom peering into the old hair salon with the sticky black tile and gold paint, what this baby's future was going to be like. By the late '90s, the new birth was so close you could feel the labor pains.

Dave, Mike, and Tom did not even have to think twice about embracing their new community. Not only was it plain common sense business-wise and in the Brick Store's best interest, it was fun becoming part of the family. City officials nudged them to meet Eddie Owen, the benevolent "godfather" of Decatur and proprietor of Eddie's Attic, the premier acoustic listening venue in the southeast. Opened in 1985, Eddie's Attic was instrumental in the Square's transformation. It's no exaggeration to say that every city pioneer sat for a spell on Eddie's outdoor patio to drink beer and envision the future. Eddie, who has seen countless young dreamers between his music venue and his former days as Trackside Tavern manager, felt the trio's distinctive professional and personal chemistry: "You could tell instantly that these boys had it together. We are so proud of what they've done."

Emilie Markert, DBA president in 1997, visited many a new business owner around that time and knew intuitively if a place was going to thrive or close shop quickly. In her opinion, it all came down to getting the "warm fuzzies" about embracing Decatur. Emilie caught a positive attitude from the minute she walked into the Pub and knew it would be a huge asset to the city. Like most of the neighborhood, she first spoke with the guys while they were chiseling plaster. Struck immediately by their friendly exuberance, she urged them to come say hello at a DBA meeting. Dave and Mike ran over from build-out, covered from head to toe in paint and sweat, with nametags slapped on dirty shirts, and said, "Hi, we're opening a pub. It's called the Brick Store." The bemused meeting attendees gave encouraging looks as the pair streamed out the door and went right back to work.

While Mike jovially blushes today when reminded of his first formal introduction as a restaurateur, at the time it spoke volumes to DBA members, who found it endearing and heartening. This young enthusiasm symbolized the realization of the community's dream, their big hope for a town renaissance. Before one official beer was sold, the Pub felt like the moment everyone was waiting for, a collective sigh that "everything would be all right" on the Square. After decades of courting a vision and local businesses falling into place, the Brick Store startup reassured them that the community would continue to grow.

As their build-out progressed, it became clear that the Pub boys had a certain reverence and enthusiasm for Decatur and everyone in it. This signified early success in the minds of other city stakeholders. Emilie's impression of Dave, Mike, and Tom underscores the Pub's anchoring impact on the business community:

> *Here they were, young boys almost right out of college . . .*
> *mature with great ideas who wanted to make it* [Decatur]
> *a better place. For them to be so young and get off to a*
> *great start, and to see beyond that and get involved with*
> *the community so early, well that's not the norm. Young*
> *people can be myopic when it comes to that. They always*
> *had a vision besides what's right in front of them, so wise*
> *beyond their years.*

Transcending the Uniform

So many different sets of folks were chomping at the bit for those young boys to open their Pub on East Court Square, yet one group remained skeptical: the City of Decatur Police Department. See, the Square was a very dark place at night back in 1997 with barely any street lights. Shadowy commercial areas makes life interesting enough for a police officer—add a bar to that equation and it could be trouble brewing.

Officer C.J. Gresham testifies to such scary conditions as he was assigned to the Square during that time. Fresh from the Clark Atlanta

University field training program, C.J. remembers patrolling two "hard drinking" bars right in the area under those dim lights. He was not overly impressed upon first meeting the Brick Store owners, an encounter that was quite unforgettable:

> *I had parked my car on McDonough and was walking up to the Square. I hear this noise like a set of blacksmiths creating some ungodly contraption. The clanking of tools, metal hitting metal, grinding. "What the hell is going on?" I'm wondering. I called the noise in to the station. It sounded like BAMB! BOOM! I remember Dave was on his knees working on something. "What are you doing?" I asked. "We're building our door." And here's this rustic door with an aged look, very classic. I'm wondering to myself, "Is this going on a Hobbit's house of J.R.R. Tolkien?" I thought, "No way. No way is this business gonna make it."*
>
> *So they told me they were building a bar on the Square. I was skeptical of it doing well. We had Grog Shop and Trackside already. I'm thinking there is no way I'm walking into a brick exterior with a wooden door. C'mon, the other store fronts had glass and steel, like Final Touch, to secure themselves. I'm thinking the product will be stolen. Plus, it seemed cheesy at the time. Antlers? Did you get those at a pawn shop? It will never make it. Then they were describing the beers they would carry, their concept, the round barrels. Okay, now I'm even more skeptical— you want me sitting around a barrel looking at a Hobbit's door. No one thought they would succeed.*

C.J. went back to the station and laughed all night with his coworkers about the Brick Store's concept and location (it's on the *Square*, aaaahhh no way!). That story quickly circled around once the wooden door opened and C.J. became a customer as well as a law enforcer and community liaison. Soon every City of Decatur police officer assigned on and around the Square became a stalwart supporter of the Pub. They told all their friends at the courthouse and brought in their sanitation worker buddies, as "here was a place that fit everybody," says C.J. The police officer continues on boundaries: "Before there was no place for everybody—the business men, lawyers, the poets, artists, and free thinkers. This place changed all that."

In the law enforcement profession, it's a given that you are always watching your back and keeping an eye on the door for the unexpected. C.J. related that in some of the bars he used to patronize, there was a high chance that he'd have to act like a bouncer. For him, the Brick Store is a haven because it's a place where he can relax and "stop acting like a cop." On a professional level, Officer Gresham deeply appreciated the open line of communication created with Dave, Mike, and Tom from the get-go, as well as their vocal support of the police department. The guys encouraged all the officers to come by and had their staff speak to them on a first name basis. In fact, once when C.J.'s supervisor popped into the Brick Store, he asked Mike how Officer Gresham was doing on his patrol duty. "Who? Oh, you mean C.J.?" It took Mike a second to associate his patron and his community liaison as an "officer" as he was part of the family. "We transcended the uniform," says C.J.

It was a simple decision, resulting in a powerful relationship that reflects the culture of Decatur. When DeKalb County police officers help staff community events on the Square, C.J. constantly hears a shocked reaction from his colleagues that goes something like this: "You mean I'm being paid to hang out, meet people, and be *thanked*? Where am I?"

Officer, you are on the Decatur Square where we always are saying, "Thank you, Brick Store Pub."

For Better or Worse: Alice

Feeling like royalty in a bar is very nice. Acting like royalty in a bar is all together different and something universally unappreciated and unacceptable in the Pub. That is unless you are a quirky, wiry, yakity, colorful, petite yet larger than life, African-American woman in her sixties by the name of Alice. Never without lipstick and earrings (and sometimes a hat), Alice was the definition of a character and a Grog Shop regular until the day it closed New Year's Eve

"An intelligent man is sometimes forced to be drunk to spend time with his fools."

—For Whom the Bell Tolls, Ernest Hemmingway

1998. Management virtually walked Alice down the street and parked her on a Brick Store barstool where she remained a fixture for ten years—three to five times a week from 3:30–4:30 and one Monday a month from one to four P.M. Her exact drink was a Screwdriver with a splash of Famous Grouse and a lemon wheel.

"Alice has a variety of outfits, all in bright colors and she lets them shine," says day bartender Todd who has been on the receiving end of the babbling matriarch's wrath if he did not make her drink perfectly right. Todd is as fond of Alice as he is infuriated by her endless talk. She gives him (and everyone else) the same speech through prescription tinted glasses: "I'm sixty-seven years old. I love you." On the day she landed in the Pub, Alice gave her barstool application to Dave, Mike, and Tom in a few short words: "I don't bother nobody." While a few souls might agree with that statement, Alice is infamous for shouting, "Hey, honey" to everyone who walks by and bugging her barkeep to "give me a splash, a splash, a splash" more of that Famous Grouse. Her simple story—that her husband is passed away, her children are grown, and she works in Dunwoody—is known by all. Some servers will give her a hug, others will avoid her like the plague, and many more will politely listen to her yammering as if they were visiting with their great auntie. Alice even inspired a waitress to come dressed as her to the Halloween party.

Not only has she been grandfathered the original Brick Store drink prices, Alice also has her own button in the computer system. On her sixty-fifth birthday (which everyone knew about three months in advance), the Pub bought her a cake, gave her cigarette money, and wrote "Happy Birthday Alice" across the bar's mirror. Before you get too chummy an impression, know that Alice has been thrown out on many occasions and has driven the owners berserk. Yet they always welcome her back, as Alice is family, for better or for worse. "There are some people who drive you so nuts that you just get past it and find some fondness for them," says Mike of his batty regular. The unfinished tale is that Alice disappeared late 2008 and no one knows what happened. So, with respects, please raise your glass and toast to the old gal and her new adventures.

As described in Part One, the Brick Store's atmosphere promotes distinctive imbibing and rich conversation. There just aren't that many Alices littered around the bar. At the same time, the management's attitude toward this special lady speaks loudly to the important character traits of understanding, acceptance, tolerance, and kindness. Perhaps forgiveness and grace as well. Grog Shop owner Jeff Trotti clearly saw the uniqueness of his new neighbors when he gave them build-out advice on how to sand the hardwood floors. A Decatur native and founding member of All Souls Fellowship, Jeff describes his old bar as "a dive" and called the Pub "a breath of fresh air with impeccable timing." Mr. Trotti shares this of the three proprietors: "They're all great guys with particularly adaptive personalities for the restaurant business. Their partnership is a good, rare combo."

The Great Decatur Beer Festival

You know a community festival has "made it" when its volunteers are on a waiting list. Such is the sensation that is the Great Decatur Beer Festival, an annual sold-out party on the Square at which 4,000 attendees drink an array of beer samples and listen to local music. Seriously, people jockey for one of the coveted volunteer slots as if beer was running out on Planet Earth. Those "in the know" gladly trade a bit of their tasting time to pour beer, run ice, or watch the entry gate because it's just so dang fun (and fifteen minutes of fame playing bartender never hurt anybody). This is a glorious five-hour long afternoon event that draws out scores of willing helpers who don't even drink alcohol—the people-watching and community vibe is that good.

Ethan Wurtzel and John Borowski of Twain's Billiards conceived of the Beer Festival in spring 1998 as a creative way to showcase amazing beer, provide beer education, and raise money for Decatur charities. "Heck yeah, we're in," said Mike when approached by the duo. Thus, the small founding committee wobbled onward "loosey goosey" and quickly enlisted help from Eddie's Attic and Trackside Tavern. Brick Store artist Jody McFerren designed a festival logo and volunteers got recruited through sign-up sheets thrown up in everyone's bar (the most names coming from the Pub). From those soggy transcripts, folks were asked to attend a meeting on Twain's patio to get a beer pouring "lesson" from Mike whose booming voice riveted the crowd as he stood on a chair and calmly shouted directions. It was less than a week to the event and the whole community was gearing up with excitement.

The first Great Decatur Beer Festival miraculously took place the day before Easter with 150 volunteers. It was a cold, cloudy, blustery

April Saturday ("colder than a well digger's bottom," says Terry Mann, Brick Store financial advisor) and the operative words may as well have been "scrambled exuberance." As several thousand people lined up at the gates, volunteers discovered a crucial forgotten item: secure money lock-boxes. Cigar boxes would just have to do, so Mike and Eddie Owen tore off in a pinch to comb these items from their establishments.

The setup crew crossed paths with the tail end of Decatur's annual holiday Easter egg hunt. Wide-eyed parents were put at ease by Mayor Bill Floyd, who never skipped a beat while explaining the ironic timing: "See, we like to have our children's Easter egg hunts and our beer festivals on the same day so families don't have to come out twice." It's a tall tale that we in Decatur enjoy recounting every year.

Decatur Square Annual Festivals

Decatur Arts Festival (Memorial Day Weekend)
Decatur Beach Party (June)
Fourth of July Festival
Decatur Book Festival (Labor Day Weekend)
Great Decatur Beer Festival (October)

Brick Store Pub Annual Events
St. Patrick's Day (March)
Pub Anniversary Party (June)
Oktoberfest Celebration (October)
Halloween Costume Contest (October 31)

Brick Store Pub Annual Staff Holidays
Big Day Out (May)
Big Night In (May)
Thanksgiving Meal (pre-Wednesday/November)
Winter Holiday White Elephant (December)

After pulling off an awe-inspiring, weather-spectacular second Beer Festival that same fall, the committee decided to permanently park the event in the month of October and take a rest. This heroic hometown feat of community organizing would have stretched the limits for any seasoned proprietor, and here was the Pub in its infancy stepping right up to the plate. Good-willed business collaboration notwithstanding, the Brick Store boys really made it all come together nicely thanks to availing the time-advantage of three partners. Mike's talent as a people-person shone as he emerged as one of the main faces of the Beer Festival. Just twenty-five years old, his leadership style was magnetic, the kind of stuff that makes you begin to understand why his favorite music performer of all time is Bruce Springsteen. Like the Boss, he leads with an inspiring combination of confidence, a generous spirit, and a universal everyday man appeal.

It's called the *Great* Decatur Beer Festival for excellent reasons that surpass a nice buzz. As the city's top fundraiser, the Beer Festival raked in a half-million dollars in 2007 that, except for a small portion, all went to charity. In fact, it received top honor in 2006 from the International Festival and Events Association, landing a first-place Gold Grand Pinnacle Award for Best Event to Benefit a Charity (Budgets under $250K). Today Mike no longer schedules volunteers by hand or juggles flimsy cigar boxes full of money in the midst of caring for his restaurant (tickets are sold online and the 350-plus volunteers are organized months in advance by the City of Decatur's designated employee Lee Ann Harvey of Volunteer Decatur). Now his favorite part is handing out fundraising checks to the selected charities and community projects at the winter DBA meetings.

Thousands descend upon the Square for the annual Decatur Beer Festival

Whether it's the Decatur Recreation Department, the YMCA, the Boys and Girls Club, a school PTSA, or the Oakhurst Recovery Program, the list of grant recipients is so long that it practically rivals the Brick Store's beer menu. Over the years, the Beer Festival monies have assisted everyone from the City of Decatur's Fire Company, Police Department, and Housing Authority, to senior citizen groups, to youth initiatives of every kind, to nature conservation and beautification interests. It even helped with a dog park pilot project. Chances are that if you're taking a rest in one of the city's green spaces or looking up at a friendly city street sign, the Beer Festival had something to do with it.

While grant checks are small, ranging from $1,000 to $5,000 dollars, they make a monumental difference to modest community non-profits. The DeKalb Rape Crisis Center (DRCC), for example, bought a building with the help of their grant money, a move that translated into a safe, secure, permanent location for survivor support and thousands of rent dollars funneled to more and better services. In two different years, a Beer Festival grant allowed DRCC to buy a laptop computer and to completely update their library (available to the public) with everything on its wish list. Thanks in part to the support of the Great Decatur Beer Festival, middle school students now receive eight weeks of lessons—instead of one day—to study what healthy, non-abusive relationships looks like.

So the next time you lay down your credit card for an event ticket and stagger into the sun and the fun with your beer-tasting glass, remember the words of Tonja Holder, former DRCC lead fundraiser:

> *We do not have to worry about this* [permanent home] *because of people like Mike Gallagher. Working in the development field, I really do appreciate business people who genuinely want to give back. The Brick Store Pub folks really have the attitude that every human being in our community deserves support. It's not just about beer drinkers or patrons or families that are well off. It's about everybody. If you look at the number of people whose lives have been positively impacted by the non-profits that this Beer Festival has helped, I'm certain the number would amaze you. It's outstanding when you look at what one can do when one is committed.*

When the Brick Store Is Your Extended Office

The orbit of the Brick Store is undeniably strong. High gravity beers aside, the gravitational force of the Pub draws in people like the Sun pulls planets. It could be a weekday in the dead of winter, just let that Georgia sky get barely warm enough (that's why we love living here) and cars automatically start pointing in the direction of the Square. Roll up to an outside whiskey barrel on an afternoon like this and you might be surprised to see who's playing extended-lunch hooky— usually an assembly of Decatur's foremost citizens, ranging from the influential to the infamous: current and former mayors, state house legislators, art curators, bank presidents, mortgage specialists, marketing executives, music studio engineers, editors-in-chief, and wild Georgian percussionists. The list goes on.

More than a few Decatur proprietors would point to the Brick Store as supportive or significant to their own success. Take the case of Rutabaga, Jon Rusnak's hair salon just a few storefronts down from the Pub. Jon opened Rutabaga just a month after the Brick Store in an old barber shop, where he immediately started trading with the guys—beer and food for haircuts. Jon found Decatur to be a great deal of fun, and he appreciated the breeziness of walking into the Pub and saying "put it on my tab." Whereas the majority of his other barter clients were stringent with money issues, the guys were straight up and easy. Alas, all good things must come to an end, as a decade later the salon owner jokes, "Now neither Mike nor Dave has hair. So now I style their wives."

Another neighborly example is Vinson Gallery, just steps away from the Pub on East Court Square from 1997–2008. Owner Shawn Vinson took one look inside the bar on his business real estate search and said, "Yep, this is our location." Shawn's knowledge of and appreciation for authentic pub culture—which is shared by his lovely British wife, the respected painter Ruth Franklin—led him to the correct presumption that he would be centering his business in a tight-knit community where folks knock off work, walk to their pub, and throw back a pint with the neighbors before suppertime. Spot on, chap. Once when Vinson Gallery hosted a showcase of lithographs from printmaker Chris Pig, Shawn took the London-based artist into the Brick Store and "dropped him off for the day" while he prepared for the show. An opportunity later arose for Mr. Pig to visit New York City, to which he informed Shawn of the jaunt, "No thanks. I'm right happy here at the Pub."

Vinson Gallery quickly became part of the Brick Store family and began showing an ongoing display of artworks on the Pub's gigantic, dark, plastered northern wall. This aesthetic addition not only enhances the sense of rustic beauty, love, and craftsmanship signature to the Pub, the display also heightens the level of conversation and community. Many a couple and cluster of friends has sparked a good-natured debate over the artistic expression that graces their fish and chips dinner. In fact, this kind of discussion is exactly how All Souls Fellowship commissioned local artist Ronnie Land to paint a work for their Decatur sanctuary hall.

Pastor Shayne Wheeler was sitting in a Pub booth with a beer like everyone else, taking in a full view of Ronnie's popular works, including the offbeat humor of *Loss Cat*. This particular piece incorporates verbiage from an actual flyer for a lost cat and juxtaposes a fully expressive feline with an endearing message about love, loss, and hope. The more Shayne absorbed of that picture especially, the more he resonated with Ronnie's style that noticeably struck a cord with Brick Store patrons. He had always felt that All Souls closely resembled the "fellowship" of the Brick Store in the way that all walks of life flow through its doors—blending different races, religious beliefs, socio-economic classes, sexual orientations, and professions.

As he pondered the parallels between *Loss Cat*, the Pub, and his pulpit, Shayne felt inspired that this artist could touch the hearts of his congregation in a similar manner as he was now experiencing. All Souls prides itself on being welcoming to everyone, and steering far away from a fundamentalist mindset, so the idea of commissioning an artist from a bar felt right in step. "We're not your grandmother's church," says Shayne.

When Ronnie heard from the pastor, he was captivated that Shayne viewed the Pub with love instead of judgment. No stranger to Southern churches, yet much more comfortable in a bar, the artist appreciated that Shayne's leaders go there, not to proselytize, but to hang out, drink world-class beer, and intermingle with the community. Ronnie humbly accepted the spiritual commission as his chance to give a "big hat's off to the Man upstairs." The resulting canvas, aptly named *Fellowship*, blossomed into an elaborate, nine-by-seven-foot, multi-colored patchwork celebrating true faith.

It's both notable and normal that Shayne met Ronnie at the Pub over a beer to discuss the project. After all, the pastor held all of his startup team conversations and dozens of other church meetings inside those four hallowed brick walls. The real truth is Shayne discovered Decatur accidentally in 2001 while brainstorming his dream location for All Souls. As Shayne talked it over on the phone with a friend, he vented his feelings of frustration about living in an isolated suburban car culture. Shayne longed to put down roots in a connected community and build All Souls in an environment where his higher self could flourish. In the meantime, he was feeling hungry, so the two friends decided to hop in their cars and meet in person for a late lunch. Shayne pulled out a metro Atlanta map and scanned it for a logical point halfway between him and his pal. "Hey, how about this place, Decatur?"

About thirty minutes later the thirty-year-old landed right in front of the Pub at a whiskey barrel table. Shayne looked around, felt the sunshine, and let the scene permeate his spirit. He saw a walkable small city with wide streetscapes, potted plants, diverse faces, and young families. He heard relaxed, familiar conversations going on amidst the afternoon bustle of the town. From the venerable brick building of the Pub itself emanated the smell of malted vinegar. Everything added up to a clear feeling of warmth and fellowship. Oh, and he had a tall, fragrant glass of Paulaner Hefeweisen sitting in front of him. Without hesitation, Shayne proclaimed to his friend, "This is home."

You might imagine from this reaction that the man had already done his research and due diligence and now was sitting down for a well-deserved beer after a long day with his Realtor. On the contrary, Shayne was bowled over by the energy of Pub and felt his soul immediately resonating with the town. Like many others who have moved to Decatur based on a Brick Store inspired hunch, Shayne's intuition told him that he'd just found his heart's desire, a community keen on the art of living. It didn't matter that he knew not a soul, the aspiring pastor was clear on this much: "I knew had to live here. I decided I would leap first and figure it out as I fell."

Shayne's next immediate task was enrolling his wife Carrie into his scheme. While touched that her partner had found a place that inspired a physical and emotional equivalent of his inner spiritual dynamic, Carrie remained practical. Just exactly how were they supposed to transplant themselves and their three children to an unknown town, raise funds to open a new church, and keep food on the table? Shayne let Decatur do the talking and took his wife on many dates around the Square. As Carrie caught the funky vibe of this quasi-artist's enclave, her musician self kicked in and she became ready to follow her heart. "Let's do it, honey. Move me and the kids to our new home, we'll figure out the rest." Like the Brick Store's ability to attract beer lovers, Shayne instantly attracted Christians who were excited with the idea of having a new community church. Everyone piled into the minister's Brick Store "office" to hear about it over a pint. Two years later, All Souls Fellowship opened their doors and according to one frequent churchgoer, "It's been a party every since."

If somehow Dave, Mike, and Tom forgot to notice that one of their regulars was a beautifully bald, unforgettably cool minister conducting follower meetings in their bar, they certainly remembered each and every Sunday morning when their staff got slammed around 11:30. All Souls services started out in the Old Courthouse, after which Shayne would shuffle the whole crowd, children and all, across the street into the Pub for lunch and bonding. Heck, the holy fermented works of Christian monks are there, so why not them? When it came time to order beverages with the waitress, the exchange got a little ecclesiastical. "What do you mean you can't serve beer before twelve noon because of church laws? We *are* the church!"

They're not the only organization that has used the Brick Store as their informal meeting space either. When Richard Lenz relocated his integrated marketing company to the Decatur Square in 1997 he wound up opening his doors the same day as the Pub (and he would go on to propose to his wife in one of their booths). Like most smart executives, Richard and his team would seek an outside environment now and again to gain fresh perspective on their vision. But unlike most in the high-rise business world, Lenz found himself in the dreamy reality of strolling down his one flight of steps and stepping into the Brick Store beehive of focused, fun energy.

As a business vendor, Lenz is quite accustomed to meeting clients at their offices. However, the agency's proximity to the renowned Pub lends a frothy advantage where prospective partners are quite willing for the mountain to come to Mohammad and meet in a cozy corner. To no great surprise, folks seem to open right up about their public relation goals while taking in the latest American, German, Belgian, or British ale sensation and listening to soul-drenched music. Hey, makes sense to me. Shouldn't all pre-planning strategy sessions look like this?

Speaking of cool music and closing deals, the Brick Store boys can add "corporate brand enhancer" to their list of accomplishments. That is, if you ask Josh Jackson and Nick Purdy, co-founders of *Paste* magazine, a national music, film, and culture publication headquartered in Decatur. Like All Souls Fellowship, *Paste* found itself starting up shop just off the Square. As the two founding media entrepreneurs sought financial backers and field recognition in 2002, they knew that their cramped, government-feeling office was not going to cut it for hosting brand-building conversations. After all, *Paste* was seeking a niche among independent-minded readers in one of the roughest industries out there—magazine publishing—in a place of which no one had heard. New York . . . Los Angeles . . . Decatur?

Josh and Nick knew it was a bit of a steep climb and so they did the most logical thing possible. They made the Brick Store into their conference room, grabbing a table whenever significant discussions needed to happen. Josh and Nick found that the specialness of the Brick Store helped explained to outsiders why they weren't picking up and moving their families to NY or LA. One sip of a Westmalle Abbey ale while listening to the music of Clap Your Hands Say Yeah on a Decatur-perfect afternoon at one of the uppermost beer bars in the nation and the future *Paste* investors seriously got it: here was the live *Paste* essence—independent and connected, authentic and accessible, conversational and substantial, cutting edge and timeless.

Josh remembers the overwhelmed reaction of his backers as they were introduced to their first McChouffe, "Wow, this is something remarkable." The cool factor kicked up several notches, as Dave Blanchard pulled out the really special stuff (a Westvleteren). The underground feel of Belgian beer discovery perfectly translated the aim of *Paste*: over delivering on cultural gems to a populace starving for different, real community.

Josh likens the Brick Store to the pub in the 1980's sitcom *Cheers*, a place where people know your name when you come in the door except they aren't pouring you a mass-produced domestic beer. "Dave will come by our booth and take a personal interest in why our guests are here. He'll ask, 'Oh, have you had this beer?' and it's always something that's going to blow their mind. It's a mystical experience," says the magazine publisher.

Josh has many reasons to say that the Pub "is the center of our community." He met his pastor here (Shayne Wheeler). As the father of three reflects on the significance of All Souls Fellowship in his life, he expands on his appreciation of the Pub as a pub. "Imagine if a pastor was afraid to come in here—oh, beer is drunk there and bad things happen here—no, great things happen here. This is where life happens." Spoken like a man who is not afraid to say he runs a rock and roll magazine and plays softball with his church.

Although the *Paste* offices are now a whole mile away, staff meetings are still held on the Square nearly every other Monday over Brunswick stew. Josh loves getting calls from his sales reps who well remember their visits to the Pub and want to know what good beer they should pick up for the Superbowl party. Once again, thank you, Brick Store Pub.

Dogwood Wake and Other Somber Gatherings

In over a decade of Brick Store days and nights, people have wandered through the doors in every kind of shape. If lonely, lost, quietly grieving, or outright sad was your flavor of the week, you can bet someone would offer you a kind word or a hug (or maybe even a tableside visit from Pastor Shayne).

"This is grain, which any fool can eat, but for which the Lord intended a more divine means of consumption... Beer!"

—Robin Hood: Prince of Thieves, Friar Tuck

That is the meaning of life and that is how life expresses itself in, as, and through this place. This is why we love the Pub.

Like beer itself, the Pub is suitable for almost every occasion, including the somber ones. Those old brick walls have witnessed many a liquid solacing among friends and loved ones over a significant loss—be that the loss of a career, a friendship, a relationship, or a family member. The last category most certainly includes four-legged children, as Deanna Greene and Molly Kesmodel will testify. When this couple lost their dog Muriel, they came to the Brick Store to cry and be together. They bumped into other folks who had lost a pet and learned of a pet crematory right in town. Thankful, the women quickly scheduled a touching service and came immediately up to the Pub to celebrate the life of their canine companion. It was a fitting location given that Deanna and Molly discovered Spatenmarzen and each other at an outside whiskey barrel many years earlier during their courtship.

Judging by the weight of all their big Brick Store discussions—moving in together, choosing paint colors, buying a second home, deciding on staying or leaving through the corporate merger, saying good-bye to dear neighbors—this couple's motto is right on: "Serious decisions, serious beer."

Atlanta-born Crawford Moran certainly knows about serious decisions. At the tender age of twenty-three he jumped into the crazy world of home brewing and never looked back. Passionate about regional beer and breweries, Crawford pushed himself to take the D.I.Y. plunge and sailed off into uncharted waters in 1996 with his first beer business venture, Dogwood Brewing Company. His specialty brews were enjoyed widely as the brew master jollily steered his way through the challenges of building a small business enterprise, which included coping with a harsh state distribution law. Said law was literally strangling the life out of his company.

One incredibly sad day, Crawford made the difficult decision to call it quits and close shop. Dogwood staff, supporters, and all independent beer lovers cried not only for the death of Decadent Ale or Whiskey Barrel Aged Barleywine, but also for the loss of a community and the end of a dream. A formal commemoration was called for.

Being of Irish blood, Crawford was certain that Dogwood's good-bye had to be a wake, that moribund custom of cheerfully raising a glass over the dearly departed and sending them off with your favorite tear-filled story. As the brewery's style had always been "one helluva good party," there was only place in town that made sense to hold an Irish wake. No question. But would the Brick Store Pub honor such a request? Without hesitation,

Michael Brian John Gallagher shot back a yes to Crawford in the form of a favorite Catholic idiom: "Does the Pope wear a funny hat?"

The Dogwood wake took place in late October 2004 complete with a makeshift casket filled with six-packs of the brewery's beer. The Pub was jammed. Every regular tap handle was pulled for the day and replaced with an all-Dogwood keg lineup. Crawford stood behind the bar, poured his beer for his Southeastern brew loving family, and got properly drunk. His father was there, a man who doesn't drink beer, and when Crawford poured his old man a third pint of Barleywine, well, that's when he knew it was a good party.

Speeches were made from the steps and every fourth song someone put "Rainbow Connection" on the CD player (yes, from *The Muppet Movie*) along with "I Like Beer" by songwriter Tom. T. Hall and various other songs about death. Nick Purdy tried to make a phone call with his car keypad, apparently opening his hatchback instead of reaching his wife. Someone even passed out on the bar. Luckily it was a once-in-a-lifetime affair thrown by the most good-natured guys on the planet who didn't mind cleaning up a few royal messes that got made (it's more than charitable when the host slips on orange rubber gloves in the middle of his own party without a word—it's grace). Everyone's favorite moment of absurdity came near the end of the night with the entire bar linked arm-in-arm, half-falling down singing, "Someday we'll find it, the Rainbow Connection, the lovers, the dreamers and me. La, la la, La, la la la."

Although some drunken revelry prevailed as expected, no one lost the point of the gathering, namely grieving Crawford's beloved brewery. It was quite sad to see the late great Dogwood laid out in sleeve holder memorial, Breakdown IPA and Decadence among many others. Dogwood was the local favorite of beer writer and aficionado Greg Nicoll who recalls this feeling at the wake: "I remember placing my scrivened condolences on a cardboard coaster and placing it into the casket on the sidewalk outside. When the lid closed, I literally felt like I was saying goodbye to an old friend."

When tragedies occur, especially those of immense scope, we need a place to come together and bond. In the bewildering hours and days following 9/11, communities sought solace with each other in pubs, bars, and other third places across America. The Brick Store was no different as Decatur communed over pints and fought for courage with the rest of the nation. It was the first time a television had ever been shown inside the building—appropriately so.

Bartender Heather Gibbons remembers standing under the skylight of the Brick Store the following day, feeling numb. In the middle of her shift, she burst out to her coworker, "We ought to do a benefit for the firefighter families." The idea caught on feverishly and, in a blink of an eye, Heather, her coworker Robert Valdez, and Shannon Barnes, the manager of Javamonkey, pulled together a benefit concert. Or rather, the idea pulled them along a Decatur jet stream, as every business and city group jumped to contribute. "Everybody wanted to do something," said Heather. "We just created the vessel."

In twelve short days, a small Brick Store committee collected donations, gathered volunteers, scheduled bands, ordered port-a-potties, and coordinated with city officials to use the Square's gazebo. A local businessman donated all 400 benefit tee shirts with the artwork penned by Brick Store cook Rian Tittle. On September 23, 2001, friends and neighbors gathered together to grieve, heal, and honor the fallen. An unbelievable $35,000 was raised that day from tee shirt sales despite a fast and powerful thunderstorm that rained out the last band and sent everyone running for cover at the Pub. The raffling continued amid a jam-packed house pushing the occupancy safety levels, but the fire marshal must have turned a blind eye just this once. Who was going to object with all of the Decatur Fire Company there passing a rubber firefighters boot for their NYC comrades?

Shannon went upstairs to count the money and felt gratefully overwhelmed as the amount kept going up and up. "It made me so proud to be a part of such a giving and caring community." As the day's events winded down, everyone who participated in the benefit felt the same salve for the soul, some throwing a kiss to the night sky as they walked out of the Pub and went home to hug their loved ones.

It's been my personal experience that the Brick Store has been the solid ground beneath my feet when Life has pulled the rug completely out from under me. The day I got the phone call from my brother that our father had thirty days left to live, I was in the Belgian Bar. It was the tail end of the March beer and cheese night, and my friend Mike Gallagher was right there to hold me up. Although this was not unexpected news

(Dad had been sick for the last two years), the impact was devastating. No one knew what to say, of course, including me. Bartender Steve tenderly offered me a beer and a quiet space enveloped around me as I sat there in disbelief. We lost Dad ninety days later on his seventy-third birthday.

Fifteen months later I got another phone call from my brother, this time from the hospital. It was a gorgeous early September afternoon and I was at the Brick Store wrapping up a book interview with Dave and his soccer teammate Jeff Hancock of Decatur First Bank. I had just bid them both goodbye and was steps away from the Square when I got the news—our mother was gone. In a state of shock I stumbled back into the Pub and flagged Dave outside. My former employer and friend of fifteen years consoled me the best he could, as I wailed on his shoulder.

My gratitude for the Pub was never as well defined as it was in those two moments. Here I was a single woman living far from home for so many years and without a drop of blood relatives anywhere south of Philadelphia. My friends, intimate relationships, and career were all in complete flux during that time period and the Pub community was just about the only certain thing in my life. I shudder to think how lost and sad I would have felt to have received that news anywhere else. Although it's quite informal, the Pub is one of my lifelines, my Decatur family tree. It's where I go when I need a hug from human arms or a red brick wall. I'm like many people living in the world without a nearby family support system. When a major life occurrence comes down the pike, it feels like skating on thin ice. This is why we need many more places like the Brick Store and the Decatur community, places that throw its arms around you when you need it the most.

For those who choose to accept it, Decatur's warm embrace can always be felt in and around the Brick Store Pub.

Life Happens in a Bar: The Birth of SkaterAid

Yes, the Pub is there for us in happy times and sad. One incredibly somber period began on Christmas Eve 2004 when a Decatur father got a phone call while at the Brick Store. His wife was relating the surreal news from the hospital emergency room that their oldest child Ian had a brain tumor. Although their fifteen-year-old son had been complaining of headaches for the last four days, this news came as a total shock. Dave stood with his friend and beloved Pub regular at the downstairs bar in compassionate, uncomfortable silence. There was nothing else to do.

Like many other kids, Ian had grown up Brick Store, occasionally sitting at the bar with dad doing his homework and perfecting the coaster flip with Ryan Gallagher. As he grew older, Ian became a skateboard fanatic and rode all around Decatur with his young friends. He felt comfortable enough to come into the Pub and ask for water on hot afternoon rides, which is perhaps why Ian asked to go to the Pub after his first chemo treatment. With the heartbreaking spunk of a child, Ian courageously pulled off his hat at the table and showed Dave his bald head, "Hey, this is me."

Yep, this was him. A beautiful, precious, vibrant teen and a gift to the Decatur community. The family felt strongly that their son would beat the odds, however Ian's strain of brain cancer was especially virulent and took his life on July 4, 2005 at nine P.M., just when the Decatur fireworks were going off over the Square. A gut-wrenching memorial service saw the boy's friends assemble together with their skateboards and tee shirts they had designed with a winged skateboard and the words "Shred for Ian." While his spirit lives forever in the hearts of his family, Ian's unique life story has also spawned a community gathering that celebrates teenagers, namely SkaterAid.

This now-annual event began from the desire of college friends of Ian's mom and dad who wanted to show their support, honor Ian, and help defray medical costs. With the help of her musician husband, Patrice Eastham got to work with Laura Deming on organizing a small music benefit. Their friend Corinne Chaves had just started Decatur Healing Arts at East Decatur Station, a contemporary mixed-use complex with a nice parking lot. Through Connie's efforts, they secured the outdoor space for the event and things began to come together. Ian enthusiastically selected a logo of Patrice's design as he and everyone else felt certain of both his attendance and his return to health.

The benefit was in the early stages of planning when the bright boy passed, and the friends tenderly asked the family if they could proceed. With a yes and a commitment of support, Ian's father pulled in his strong network of community contacts. Thus the event evolved into something different. Instead of just a fundraiser to help defray medical expenses, it became a way to celebrate Ian's life. SkaterAid took off with the inspiration of the winged skateboard and became what it is today: a kid-friendly, long September afternoon complete with teenage bands, skateboard competition, prizes, fried foods, face painting, and auctioned art (most appropriately done on recycled skateboard decks). All proceeds benefit families dealing with pediatric cancer.

Along with Thomas Taylor's Stratosphere Skateshop, Patrice credits the Pub's Carol Blanchard with making the event happen every year, describing her support as indispensible and essential to building the character of the event. Pub manager Kelley Turner assisted Ian's school pal Sam Eastham with the raffle that first year and has grown to be a core member of the SkaterAid team. Through Sam's connection with Kelley, he got himself a dishwashing job at Brick Store once he turned eighteen. Becoming part of the Brick Store family was a great experience for Sam and gives his mother Patrice another reason to be grateful.

"Every year it seems that the Brick Store has become more integral to SkaterAid, from Carol and Kelley's participation from the start to Dave's support of the art auction and that amazing pre-auction breakfast in the Belgian Bar. It's become impossible to separate the Pub from SkaterAid—they are fundamentally tied together." Patrice continues on the theme of love at the Pub:

> *It is so appropriate* [this title] *because there is such a generosity of spirit in that place, and I think that spirit is a big part of why the Brick Store has become such a central gathering place for the Decatur community. It really brings back the historical idea of the pub as a community resource and a home away from home.*

Laura Deming shares the impact of SkaterAid and why she loves volunteering: "I'm inspired to keep co-leading SkaterAid because of the feedback we get from kids. Our biggest fans are 12-18-year-olds who say it's the only event in Decatur geared towards their age group. We've even nurtured some budding young Decatur musicians." Laura appreciates the Pub's annual beer donation and event promotion efforts, fondly recalling the sight of thirty-plus art skateboards displayed on the Brick Store's northern wall. Then there's the fact that she can count on many of the Pub's employees and loyal customers as their most reliable volunteers (including a soaking wet appearance by server Cozmo in the dunking booth).

As for the Brick Store community as a whole, Ian's brave fight touched a deep cord with many Pub goers who remembered the essence of family and love at the Pub shining through during that time. One such person was Pastor Shayne Wheeler whose own child had been brushed by leukemia. At one point someone close to Ian's family asked Shayne if he would step downstairs from his balcony table to visit with the father and offer him words of comfort. It was irrelevant that he was not the man's minister or that Shayne was in the middle of enjoying his beer; this was the Pub, Decatur's tight-knit third place. As one long-time regular has observed, "life happens in a bar."

SkaterAid's integral relationship with the celebratory and nurturing culture of the Brick Store is well summed up in the event's website description: "Ultimately, SkaterAid is a place for teens to celebrate their youth. Whether flying through the air on a board, playing music, or hanging out with friends, you're only fifteen once in your life, so . . . skate on. And shred for Ian."

Halloween: "We Don't Serve Robots in Here!"

If spooky, incognito, or outlandish is your speed, then by all means don a wig and go hide under the Pub's eerie candelabra for their annual Halloween party. Be prepared not to recognize anyone or anything, as brick walls transform from cozy to ominous. Grab a Rogue Dead Guy Ale and catch a good seat for the spectacle of people in costumes parading down the stairs to compete for the big cash prize. You'll see everything from pregnant nuns to grumpy old men, to Al and Peg Bundy, to Trekkies, to Amelia Earhart, to Evel Knievel and his Naughty Nurses, to Edward Scissorhands, to dominatrix ballerinas, to "that guy who is a . . . well, we don't know what he is," as one partygoer observed (he was the cartoon character MC Scat Kat from the Paula Abdul music video "Opposites Attract").

You know it's a great party when you feel like you're on a Hollywood set or when the get-ups confound the mind, like the Pub's graphic artist coming as a "one night stand." And who was that big, clunky, pink robot that (teasingly) got refused service? Honestly, this party goes over best with staff and regulars who love letting loose for an outrageous holiday. "Halloween is my favorite time of the year," shares Emory University employee Cathy Keeler, who views the Pub as the beating heart of Decatur. Cathy says she keeps coming back because the owners are so clearly invested and they know their patrons (well, maybe not on All Hallows Eve). Cathy has entered the costume contest for over five years, her sparkling dark eyes bringing mischievousness to the personas of dark angel, cowgirl, and skull creature. "It's the best Halloween party and contest because their standards are so high. I usually gather a big crowd to come up. It totally lets you step outside of yourself for a little while and get wild."

Owner Mike Gallagher completely agrees that it's a time "where you get to be a kid again and do whatever you want," He loves judging the Pub's costume contest because people throw themselves into it with gusto, much like Mike himself. As evidenced by his own Halloween costumes, which typically heavily favor movie and TV characters, Mike has gone all out to become Austin Powers, the Godfather, the Ladies Man from *Saturday Night Live*, and Arthur ("I looked nothing like Arthur, but I had so much fun playing like Dudley Moore"), and even as actors themselves, such as Jack Nicholson and Christopher Walken. No one can touch Mike when it comes to staying in character, such as the year he came as Irish gypsy Mickey O'Neill from the movie *Snatch* and confounded everyone by babbling incomprehensibly for the entire evening. Hey Brad Pitt, watch your back!

Mike Gallagher as the Godfather

As a bar proprietor, Mr. Gallagher is particularly tickled that they get to throw such a fun gig in their establishment. "It's one of those things you'd just want to do if you owned your own place." In fact, "Why not throw a party?" was the exact reasoning of the "three amigos" when they decided to slip on matching ponchos and host the first Brick Store Halloween bash. Dave, Mike, and Tom continued as a threesome the following year, as the Three Musketeers (in gorgeous blue capes). That bond soon broke down and the Blanchard clan wowed the crowd when Dave and his wife Talia conscripted some willing pals and their Great Dane Agnes to be Scooby Doo and his gang. "Dave insisted we dye Aggie brown [for maximum Scooby Doo-ness], but she turned out red and stained everyone who touched her," remembers a chagrined Talia.

Dave would offer affable post-party apologies again several years later when he and Brad Zimmerman imitated sleazy '70s disco dancers just a little too well. ("Hey, you wanna dance wid *me*?") The humorous truth is no one really cared. In fact the Pub kids were impressed. But, what's a family without a little merciless ribbing, like the year Twain's owner and Blanchard brother-in-law Ethan Wurtzel gathered a trio of his own and came as the spitting image of the three Pub owners. Great one, Ethan!

To restate the facts, restaurant work is a physically, mentally, and emotionally taxing job. Add copious amounts of nightly alcohol consumption by the public and it can sometimes feel like babysitting or worse. So it's imperative for a thriving, functioning bar staff to kick back and bond through plain, silly fun such as the Pub staff does on a night like Halloween.

One year, every cook, server, and bartender came as Mike Gallagher. Many were dressed in Mike's actual trademark hats and shirts, which his brother Ryan had quietly pilfered from his house. The Pub was a vast sea of black mustaches (many pasted on), Gatsby caps, and short-sleeved collared pullovers that screamed a very fond *gotcha* for this dear jovial man who himself is a master teaser.

That same night, Tom was a surprise hit as he dressed in the identical image of one of his employees, cook Rian Tittle. The likeness was uncanny: a mesh, wide-brimmed baseball cap, a pack of cigarettes rolled up in a white tee shirt, painted-on tattoos all down his arms, hair slicked back, and a full beard. Tom even got the man's wiry smile down pat. Someone dragged Rian out of neighboring Twain's, telling him, "Dude, you've got to go up to the Brick Store and see who's posing as you." Imagine the shocked look of the quiet fish-n-chips slinger as he walked out the Pub's back door only to see himself portrayed by the man who writes his paychecks. So many owners barely know the person behind the apron who makes their restaurant work and succeed. This was sly homage at its finest, it almost made you want to sing a version of Bonnie Raitt's "Something to Talk About."

Er, we don't exactly mean *that* kind of talking—except if you mean Tom's respectful love for Rian's mother, Mrs. Janice Tittle. Every year she sends a Halloween confection care package to her son that includes a mound of peanut brittle for everyone to share. The Brick Store kids obsess for weeks about this mouthwatering, melted, sugary, fresh-out-of-a-Valdosta-Georgia-oven homemade treat. When that famous "Tittle Brittle" brown paper package lands on the downstairs bar, the bosses actually takes a number and stand in line behind the rest of the staff. Talk about grown up children! Mrs. Tittle is royalty in everyone's eyes, even receiving a thank you poinsettia one year from the managers, although Rian is adamant about his 70-year-old mother's retirement.

We'll see.

Back to the likes of Nosferatu and his sexy vampire victim (former Brick Store bartenders and marriage partners Brad and Susan Zimmerman) . . . a huge number of former and current Pub staff love to come to this party dressed to the nines—or Nine Inch Nails rather. No one dressed with more zeal than Brick Store's first hired employee, Robert Valdes, who would sometimes start his costume in January. He won grand prize a *whoop-assing* three times, although not for his clever rendition of "a can of whoop-ass."

Over the years, Roberto has come down the Pub steps to thunderous applause as a member of rock band KISS (his sweet coworker Smiling Al trading her soft countenance to become a fiercely painted, full-tongue out Gene Simmons), Schneider from the '70's hit TV series *One Day at a Time*, something fantastic from the science fiction movie *Tron*, iconic journalist Hunter S. Thompson, exercise fanatic Richard Simmons, and a risqué "film star" from *Girls Gone Wild* (seriously, you don't want a description of this one).

There was not a trace of nepotism the year that Dave's eighteen-year-old nephew, Wes, took first place for his portrayal of Michael J. Fox's movie character in *Teen Wolf.* Not only did the kid cover himself in fur and howl down the steps with style, Wes also made a dramatic entrance by surfing atop the "Wolfmobile" van driven by Teen Wolf's best friend Stiles (driven in real life by Wes' best friend Daniel Gordy). Dave let out a gasp as the Wolfmobile cruised into the cul-de-sac and careened the corner landing a fuzzy Wes in front of the Pub's door. Glad you're still with us, Teen Wolf (and Stiles too, as the pals are currently employed in the kitchen and needed for their shifts). Kids, do *not* try this at home!

Another Brick Store staff first place prize went to longtime Pub server Greg "Gerg" Bromfield for an amazing homemade stingray costume. His tall frame encased in a seven-foot cardboard wingspan covered with plush, marbled fabric and complete with mesh eyes and a tail, Gerg was a huge hit with fellow carousers. As the stingray floated through the night's proceedings with dead-on marine life precision, waving his fins and gently flattening his body on top of car hoods parked out front, you thought you were at the Georgia Aquarium.

Honorable Pub family mentions go to Ryan Gallagher as a perfect Popeye and twice as Eddie Munster (the second time to accompany the Blanchard gang as the entire Munster family), yours truly (Mary Jane Mahan) for nine years in blue spandex as "MJ" Spiderwoman, Pub staff for collective representation as "Boogie Nights" (now that's drinks served with a smile), and Shannon Barnes as "the Brick Store" (we've never seen a woman make a red brick wall costume look so good).

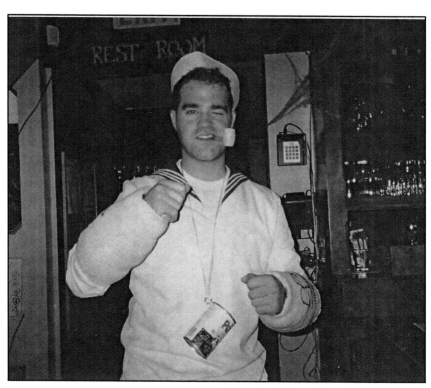

Pub manager Ryan Gallagher as Popeye

Let's not forget the year Blake Guthrie brought down the house dressed simply as "Coach" in high spandex shorts, cap, whistle, and a clipboard. The fact that Blake won two other Halloween contests on the Square that same night as your average parent coach speaks well to the spirit of Everyday Joe or for anyone who yearns to lead, be it a business, a city council, or, yes, a youth athletic team. As renowned football coach Vince Lombardi once said, "Confidence is contagious and so is lack of confidence, and a customer will recognize both."

A befitting wrap-up to this party is an image of Mike at the top of the stairs in 2007 in character as Jack Nicholson. As the costume pageant began to come down the steps for judging—"Jack" announcing every entry—the Grim Reaper started to pound the bejeezus out of the steps with his scepter. While it made a menacing impression on the crowd, the thumping was also imperiling the handmade wooden steps. The pride of the entrepreneur broke through Mike's character as "Jack" told the Grim Reaper in a smooth yet threatening tone, "Hey, we built that ourselves. Watch it."

More Brick Store Bashes

Parties and gatherings, like beer, can be marked by the seasons. Halloween is a pleasant endnote to autumn that has seen an entire month of celebrating the spirit of Oktoberfest, the jolly and famous sixteen-day German event held in Munich. In contrast, the Brick Store's Bavarian fare blesses only one afternoon, but it's a good one, ach ja? This suds-filled Saturday officially kicks off in strict Oktoberfest tradition, namely with the town mayor (Bill Floyd) tapping the Märzen keg. One year when the Decatur chief magistrate was unavailable, Dave enrolled German-born-and-raised Volkmar Wochatz for tapping duties. It would have been better for Dave to rope in a monkey, as Volkmar was mortified at this "break of mayoral custom." Nonetheless, he popped in the spout perfectly to the sound of a roaring, thirsty crowd. Mr. Floyd, on the other hand, felt a tad relieved as he always sweated out the swinging of the wooden mallet. "I just hope one year I don't bust it open and make it all foam out," he humbly smiles. Well, Bill, we know this wasn't on the job description, so all we can say is *danke*.

In Volkmar's words, this is a *gemütlich* afternoon or a slow, comfortable, relaxed drinking session that sees an enormous brew-filled Ayinger boot passed around and around the horseshoe bar. Folk's eye up the boot as it approaches them, ready to polish it off with a victory cry of "das gute bier!" It would be tempting to presume that the pixie-like waif seated next to you could not possibly even hold this heavy stein, let alone finish it. Hold your Gäsmbart hats, gentlemen, as a lass will always surprise you with how much beer she can put in her belly. Better yet if she's dressed appropriately in a Dirndl (bodice and apron) and leading German drinking songs, a sight for which we can thank Pub regular and beer aficionado Lance Deen. Realtor by day, Lance rallies a Lederhosen gang every Oktoberfest clad in traditional Bavarian leather knee-britches costume, even bringing infant son Luke dressed in mini-lederhosen made by Grandma (what a way for a tyke to start off life, steeped in culture).

December is lovely in Decatur with its "mallternative" local shopping options that see plenty of folks belly up at the Brick Store for their yearly Christmas pint of Sierra Nevada Celebration Ale. A classic and hoppy winter seasonal, the Celebration Ale is a rarity like Santa Claus as the Sierra Nevada brewery no longer makes a regular appearance on the Pub tap handles. "Sierra Nevada is excellent, and they always have been, but we now tend to promote smaller craft breweries that are less accessible," Dave says of the craft industry leader. Nevertheless, he gets his Celebration fill at the Brick Store staff holiday party where coworkers enjoy a night off relaxing and visiting with each other over gift exchanges that range from tasteful to unmentionable.

American IPA (Sierra Nevada Celebration Ale): IPA stands for Indian Pale Ale. It contains typically American hops with a big herbal and/or citric character and high bitterness. It is moderate-to-medium-bodied with a balancing malt backbone. Very pale golden to reddish amber in color. A different soul from reincarnated IPA style, first brewed in England and exported for British troops in India during late 1700s. To withstand the voyage, Pale Ales were tweaked to become a much more malty, higher alcohol content, well-hopped IPA (hops are a natural preservative). Historians believe IPAs were watered down for the troops, while officers and the elite savored it at full strength.

On December 31, the Brick Store Pub joins the rest of the restaurant and bar industry with a good old fashioned New Year's Eve countdown. It's not the place to "get your freak on" if you like it wild. Rather the tone is "nice people go there," says Emilie Markert. She recalls chatting with a visiting couple from Indiana who came to Atlanta just for a music concert. Also home brewers, they had researched the Pub (then at #3 on BeerAdvocate.com) and took the MARTA train to Decatur for an authentic Brick Store experience and a sweet start to their holiday festivities.

Original Pub regulars and longtime couple Steve and Diane Bradshaw were delighted to spend several NYE countdowns at the Brick Store. Diane never forgets the year that Mike got up and gave them his table at Booth One because it was so crowded. In reality, this amateur party is just another great Pub outing for the Bradshaws who used to meet for date night every Friday to have those special, private, intense conversations that wouldn't happen during the week. Steve and Diane, who recognize the high turnover rate in most places, appreciated being greeted by a friendly nucleus of bartenders and servers during their long stretch of time at the Pub. Like many other regulars, they applauded the success of the Brick Store and lamented for themselves when it was no longer a snap to get an empty seat. They simply got creative and changed the time of their visits. For this easy-going couple, a busy NYE or Friday afternoon at the Pub is worth the effort because "you feel like you're a part of it because the guys share it."

Well said, Diane. Nice seeing you and the hubby on many a St. Patrick's Day, understood locally as "A Brick Store Holy Day of Obligation." No worries, Father Gallagher will not be asking you for the date of your last confession (unless perhaps you're trying to weasel a staff Jamison shot). However you can bet a green kiss on the Blarney Stone that March 17 *is* the day for Celtic tradition to ring loud at the Pub as the Irish flag hangs from the balcony. Kitchen staff pumps out corn beef, cabbage, and mashed potatoes until they drop while bartenders pour Guinness until their arms fall off. It's a wonderful day.

As long as the weather holds, a few tables get put out on the sidewalk so fiddlers can entertain inside with traditional Emerald Isle ballads. The boys learned an important lesson regarding authentic Irish music on their first St. Patrick's Day in 1998 when they let the staff house band play. Somehow the group name of "Just Puppets" didn't ring very Irish nor did their musical covers of funk artist Prince. Michael Gallagher was in hot water for a minute, as his Uncle Joe had travelled all the way from Philadelphia for his nephew's party and was not having one bit of this "shite nonsense." Almost booting Robert Valdez's arse out of the Pub's window area, Uncle Joe grabbed the microphone and delivered "O Danny Boy" a cappella in a way that would have made Saint Brigid cry. In fact most eyes were misty with both love and relief as the Gaelic-looking man channeled Ireland's heartbeat, bringing its beauty alive in the Pub. Oh Uncle Joe, thank you for your smiling Irish eyes.

Let's turn this over to patron Robin Tanner who never misses a St. Patrick's Day with husband Byron Finley:

> *I love the pub because it is a place of comfort and happiness. It has helped us stay married because it's one of our places we both love and always enjoy. Having gone to Ireland for our honeymoon, we can appreciate the value and uniqueness of a true neighborhood pub. Although I was eight months pregnant this year for St. Pat's [2009], Mike still gave me a tiny sip of whiskey so this boy can come out Irish!*

A Love Supreme: Weddings at the Pub

Showing up for success takes on profound meaning when it refers to the institution of marriage. This isn't glancing at a lengthy beer list and saying, "I guess I'll take that one." This is your opportunity to knock the ball out of the park regarding one of life's greatest commitments, where the joys and challenges of matrimony officially kick off upon an exchange of rings. For many a couple, the wedding day is remembered as one of the most special events in their lives. What a lovely and heartfelt testimony is it then that a few dozen brides and grooms have gotten engaged or tied the knot in and around the Brick Store Pub. It's a perfect match, really, if you consider that any pair serious about their vows would love for both their union and their wedding day to be described in the same way we think of the Brick Store—namely as special, warm, authentic, and committed.

Considering the stress and expense of throwing an all-out affair (especially if immediate relatives might not exactly be the Walton family) many couples throughout the ages have opted for *easy, casual,* and *relaxed* matrimonial ceremonies. If you're going to keep it small and call a judge anyway, why not take your betrothed where there's already an ever-present feeling of love, the heart of Decatur's downtown community? Besides, if the bride has the jitters, you can easily ply her with a nearby whiskey (most likely at her request). Minus the pre-wedding shot, that's precisely what Emily and Brent Kandetzki did back on June 30, 2000. Emily remembers:

> *We'd been friends and coworkers for over two years. We'd gone on lunch dates, out drinking, played pool, hung out in each other's offices. I called him one day, bored, hoping he'd catch a movie with me and found myself nervous about it. He called back and said he'd go. We saw an 80-minute movie in the theater, and I walked out thinking, 'Wait! This can't be over yet!' He was driving me home and I was desperate for the date not to end. I suggested we get a drink at the Brick Store. The rest is history. We moved in a month later and we were married five months after that.*
>
> *We knew our wedding was going to be a small affair. We called the DeKalb County judge and asked him to meet us at the Brick Store, the site of our first date. The bar said it would be fine to have our ceremony there. However, the judge suggested we go outside since the day was beautiful. We got married under a big tree on the Square. One of the Brick Store managers was kind enough to join us and take pictures. She was the only attendant at the ceremony! Of course, we went to the Pub afterwards.*

Eight years later, as this husband and wife closed in on yet another happy anniversary, a different set of spouses took their place at the horseshoe bar to celebrate vows. It was a lovely spring afternoon, none other than Earth Day, April 22. The Pub felt nearly half full and fabulous. Sunlight streamed in the door and through the skylight and windows, and the warm air smelled fresh after a much-needed hard rain the night before. Bob Weiler sat relaxed and unassuming, perched along "pro row" (those first few stools next to the beer cooler) with a good-looking draught of Konig pilsner in front of him. A handsome and distinguished gentleman with salt-and-pepper hair and a blue suit, Bob just might have blended in with the eclectic crowd if it weren't for a more stunning sight of the woman by his side, his new bride, Lisa Pealer. Looking gorgeous and utterly conspicuous in her white silk dress, Lisa radiated the happiness and peace attributable only to a woman who'd just eloped and was now seated in the best reception-hall-for-two on Earth.

Bob and Lisa, both in public health careers at the University of Florida and the Centers for Disease Control and Prevention respectively,

"The mouth of a perfectly happy man is filled with beer."

—Egyptian Proverb

had enjoyed a long distance courtship across state lines. This included many trips to the Brick Store, a welcome respite from the limited bar choices splattered across Gainesville (typical sports bars with multiple TVs, wings, loud music, and college students). All "anti-Brick Stores," as Bob proclaimed. The travel-loving duo imagined taking an extended honeymoon in Italy but knew this would be impossible to pull off if they took on the expense of a traditional wedding or a destination wedding—even if it was a small wedding.

Although it would be a first marriage for both of them, the couple strongly resonated with two key ingredients of elopement: its practicality and its *non*-traditional nature. After all, here were two level-headed individuals in their late thirties and early fifties, already possessing their own blenders and food processors, prepared to live in different towns after saying the "I dos" until new jobs were sorted out. If you were voting on their choice of registering at Macy's or four weeks exploring the likes of Vatican City and Cinque Terre, what lever would you pull?

Yep, you'd send Bob and Lisa straight for real Italian pasta and march them down the aisle of the DeKalb County courthouse for easy and effortless nuptials (well, they did have to feed five dollars of quarters into the parking meter, bless their hearts). After an emotional ceremony, the newlyweds made a beeline to the Brick Store to enjoy a few Konigs and the serenity of each other's company.

Actually, Lisa had made a special request for manager Kelley Turner to be working that day. After getting to know Kelley through some great afternoon sessions in the Pub, a very excited Lisa broke down and confided girl-to-girl to her bartender about the secret plans (the ones she hadn't even told her mom yet, even though the date was in less than six weeks). It was to be a courthouse wedding and some lunch and beers at their favorite spot. Would she please be there to celebrate? Kelley not only responded yes, she immediately offered to make one of her famous cakes, a scrumptious triple-layer double-chocolate fudge cake with raspberry ganache, whipped cream filling, and cream cheese raspberry frosting (so sorry, but that's not on the regular menu).

When asked, Lisa reflected on her nervousness about the big day despite the lack of planning hoopla: "The Brick Store was the light at the end of the tunnel that would make it all okay." While confident in their decision to elope, the range of emotions that went along with that decision did not escape Lisa and Bob. They simply did not alter the course. "We really try to stay focused on what is important to us and not to get distracted by the other stuff. I think that is the same philosophy with the Brick Store, which is why its aesthetic is so appealing to us," said Lisa.

The groom had been a fan of the place ever since the love of his life brought him through that wooden door while on their courtship. Already his wife's biggest fan, this perfect move—a few good, cold Konig pilsners at the Pub and a simple celebration dinner with family and friends—had Bob put this woman straight into angel status. As the informal crowd gathered at the Brick Store feasted on the abundance of homemade wedding cake, Michael Gallagher chatted up the happy couple, eyes full of love for this blessed expression of humanity. "To see a bride and groom come celebrate their most special day in your pub, sitting at your bar—that just makes a man proud."

For the record, Mike gets to beam with pride at least two dozen times a week in his Pub. About forty dozen, if you include the scenes of life he doesn't directly witness, such as the Gillespie-Thurston wedding party, two newly united families who spent the better part of their weekend making memories at the Brick Store. First they closed down the bar after the formal wedding rehearsal. Then they returned to the Pub post-wedding reception and watched the proud father of the bride in full tuxedo asking for quiet around a whiskey barrel, pint in hand, so he could make an announcement: "Everyone—I want to introduce you all to Mr. and Mrs. . . . um . . . er . . . what's your last name now?" Seeing Dad relax and tip a few back with the family was really nice. It tied a bow on a perfect wedding weekend. Years later what guests would remember most about that event was (no surprise) their time spent in the Pub.

There are whirlwind engagements—and then there are engagements that turn into whirlwinds. Like the night of March 14, 2008, when Brick Store regular Kevin Donovan proposed to his wife Heidi in a snug Pub booth as a severe tornado ripped the roof off the Georgia Dome and devastated a historic downtown Atlanta neighborhood that was home to two Pub inner-circle members. With heartfelt prayers for all who were adversely affected by the storm, Mike Gallagher was thankful that this act of nature didn't steal the show. He had worked for over 48 hours with Kevin to pull off an imaginative scheme to give his fiancée the surprise of her lifetime. Kevin hatched a plan where he would pop the question in the richness of the Brick Store Pub via their large drink chalkboard.

The synchronicity gods smiled generously upon Kevin the day he stepped forward to ask Mike for help. He called and got through to him at the precise moment Mike and Dave were in the basement storage room locked in a heated debate on whether or not to put the scotch and whiskey chalkboard *back* up after a long hiatus. Mike literally had the board in his hands and was shaking it passionately while stating his pro-restoration argument to his partner, who held the opposing view, when the phone rang. Their nervous and loyal patron's "big daddy" request ended the discussion quickly. When a man tells you that he's found a woman who's the "sanctuary of himself," someone he can go to like a place—like our revered Pub—and know all is right with who he is, well, another happily married man steps up fast to help make that dream come true. Dave agreed for the chalkboard's return with the debut announcement: HEIDI WILL YOU MARRY ME?

The chalkboard was hung high on the brick wall that Friday and the staff held their collected breath as Heidi and Kevin showed up. There was a definite chill in the March air, and the statuesque brunette became slightly irritated with her beau for insisting they sip their pre-dinner pints outside instead of in the cozy, crowded waiting area. Kevin and Mike both braced themselves as things almost fell apart when Heidi excused herself to go to the ladies' room. Miraculously, she never looked up, although Heidi vaguely remembers sensing a strange intensity coming from the proprietor as she exited the door. "He was a flurry of small talk and his face was a tad flushed as if he was sweating."

Hey, Heidi, here's the deal. Mike loves people. He loves his regulars. He loves love. He loves life and all those who choose to live it boldly. He's also a man of tradition who just the year prior majorly sweated out proposing to the love of his life—as any guy should—while on the rocky coast of Ireland. He was as jittery as your husband to get you out of that bar so Kevin could deliver the goods as planned. You weren't supposed to go to the bathroom.

Heidi felt relieved to have Mike finally seat them at their table, her mood damp, like the weather they'd just left outside. The hungry woman glanced down at her menu and paid little attention to the man inwardly squirming across from her. That's when Kevin made his move, asking, "So, what do you think of the drink selections tonight?"

In a surreal moment, Heidi looked up to the illuminated chalkboard, saw her name scrawled in large capital letters with the conversation question of all time, and suddenly put both hands to her cheeks in a sincere McCauley Culkin *Home Alone* gesture.

Kevin proudly produced a diamond ring and moved swiftly to his sweetheart's side of the booth. As Heidi clasped his hands and Mike brought out an ornate Belgian bottle of Deus (a champagne-like beer) and two flutes, Kevin indeed knew that all was right in his world.

The new Mrs. Donovan affectionately recalls that only her father and stepmother knew of the upcoming proposal at the time. Sure, just them, Kevin, Mike, and an entirely packed house three nights running at the Brick Store wondering, "Who the heck is Heidi?"

Bière de Champagne (Deus) One of the newest and most interesting styles with much crossover potential as a top-shelf beer. Primarily brewed in Belgium, this beer undergoes a lengthy maturation and a "methode de champenoise" (remuage and dégorgement) process of removing yeast from the bottle—basically the same bottle conditioning that actual Champagne goes through. Some are even cave-aged in the Champagne region of France. Most are delicate, high in alcohol, highly carbonated, and sometimes spiced. Colors range from very pale to dark hues.

Among other nuptial conversation starters, how about that couple who waltzed into the Pub at 5:15 on a day in May, preacher in tow, and asked if they could throw the man of the peace behind the bar and get hitched. Apparently these two lovebirds had met the year before on this same day, at this exact time, at the very barstools where they were now kindly gesturing for the patrons to move over so their minister could perform a five- minute ceremony. The bartender slid over a few steps, witnessed the event, gave them a beer, and we haven't seen the couple since. We'll blame it all on the St. Bernardus 12.

While it warms the heart to see anyone say, "I do," the Brick Store family of staff has delighted time and time again to be present at weddings of their inner circle, many of whom met their spouses while working together at the Pub. Under the most intimate of circumstances, the Pub once closed for the marriage of two special folks, Melissa and Chris Langley, whose service was performed by longtime bartender Ben Karp.

Melissa and Chris, early hires on the guys' payroll, were a young couple starting out in life when they made a humble request to their employers to join hands in matrimony under the bar skylight. It was 1998 and the Brick Store's magic was still a great secret, meaning the guys were more than fine with disappointing a handful of patrons so they could watch their darling "Mel" float down the steps as a vision in white. Forget bottom-line financial decisions, this was an honor. Besides, the entire staff was invited so there was no one to work if the couple held the ceremony elsewhere.

Coming full circle, Ben would meet his own wife a few years later while tending bar. As a single woman, Elizabeth loved the Pub due to the fact that she could come in by herself and not have to worry about unwanted advances, including her smitten bartender. A consummate professional, Ben never approached her for more than a drink order, which he would have waiting for Elizabeth before she took her barstool (Sandeman 20 year old port).

One night a group of Pub servers went to see a music concert and Elizabeth tagged along, as she had an interest in the band. This presented Ben the opportunity to ask her out, which led to "the most perfect date ever" at a fantastic Italian restaurant (The Patio, now defunct) followed by a drink at the North Highland Pub. Elizabeth shocked Ben by first ordering a Guinness (his pint of choice) and then by sharing a puff of his Cuban cigar, which he had saved for a special occasion. Conversation flowed right up to the polite goodnight kiss Ben landed on her cheek. The man was smitten . . . and called her the very next day for another date (uh-oh).

"Um, I'll see. I don't know what's going on. Call me Thursday," Elizabeth replied. Feeling shot down and heartbroken, Ben took the hint and didn't call her. He assumed a cordial air when she came into the Pub and never alluded to their date, mustering a cool "Toodles" when she left (Ben's customary patron adieu). For the next three months Ben suffered this pretend game with a gut feeling that she could be "the one." Hedging his bets, Ben apparently hopped the bar on New Years Eve 1999 and delivered a midnight kiss to his elusive lady friend (close friends swear "the hop" happened, although Elizabeth and Ben laughingly protest otherwise). Hopeful Ben lived with rejection and regret as he poured many more pints of Guinness for his beloved and as she again put an ocean of distance between herself and the man behind the bar.

After a few months, a friend informed Ben that Elizabeth secretly favored her barkeep. However, she liked her barstool at the Pub more and feared estrangement from her treasured watering hole if a dating relationship went south. Ben quickly assuaged the woman's fears of getting involved with her bartender and told Elizabeth, "I am in no rush. You know how I feel. You've got my phone number and it ain't over till the fat lady sings." He did not wait long before his phone started ringing. Soon enough Ben and Elizabeth were together and engaged (on a gondola in Italy). They married a year later.

Ben became a minister in the early '90s while he was playing in a rock band and took his duties quite seriously, performing a total of five weddings. Certified through an Internet application to the Universal Life Church in California, Ben was not the only online ordained barkeep in Decatur. He shared great company with everyone's favorite Twain's fixture Paul Weaver, a damn fine bartender at that establishment since 1998. Paul's ministerial client list is heavily weighted with Brick Store Pub couples including top-of-the-Pub-list Dave and Talia Wurtzel Blanchard (1999), who held a lovely reception at the Pub, as well as

Mike and Erin Stone Gallagher (2007), who made an indelible mark on the Serenbe Inn organic farm grounds in Palmetto, Georgia.

Brick Store manager Ryan Gallagher, Mike's younger brother, gladly exchanged rings with his beloved wife Emily in front of Paul under the soft glowing lights of the Le Moulin Rouge reception hall stage on April 15, 2006. In an interview, Ryan smiled wide as he explained the ironic timing. "I figured I might as well pick a date to forever remind me where all my money was going—Uncle Sam and my wife."

Ryan first laid eyes on Emily as she sat in a Brick Store booth having dinner with a friend. Her brother-in-law delivered the U.S. mail to the Pub and constantly raved about the place. When Emily decided to check out the fuss for herself, her vivacious presence quickly stirred up a friendly competition among the male cooks and servers who vied for her attention. Smart, determined man that he is, Ryan edged out his restaurant brothers and won her over (although Emily swears it was the four Aventinus ales she was served that got him the phone number).

The exact same scene had played out a few years earlier when Davis Petterson came out of the Pub's kitchen for a break and spotted an adorable female guest deep in conversation. Christy Bardis was intent on finishing her article for the now defunct *Community Review* "Hot Plate" section, but not too busy to notice the fresh-faced young jazz drummer covered in fish beer batter who was now smiling at her tableside. Maybe it was the Sweetwater IPA or perhaps it was just the cook's sweet intentions. At any rate sparks flew and Christy and Davis went on to stake their claim as husband and wife in 2002.

For Christy and Davis, Paul once again assumed a sacramental role when an intimate wedding party gathered close together under the Decatur Square gazebo. Tradition mingled with special touches, as an Episcopal prayer book reading gave way to the *Acknowledgement* track of John Coltrane's "Love Supreme." Before heading to a small reception at That Pottery Place, family gazed at a Marc Chagall painting whose depiction of lovers floating through the sky connoted a dreamy picture of Davis and Christy.

Paul had to put on his best officiate face and bite back the urge to whistle at the groom when cook Ed Morris showed up for his wedding in a Scottish kilt (2005). Ed's enchanting bride, server Brooke Dailey, joined her man in a surreal moment of beauty and led the entire room of guests in a soft rendition of "Tonight You Belong to Me," a classic ukulele tune first made famous by Steve Martin in the movie *The Jerk*. Just about every person who ever worked at the Brick Store with Ed and Brook attended the lovely affair held in The Solarium at Historic Scottish Rite on that perfect afternoon, buzzing with wine and humming along with the sounds of love.

Of all the marriage services led by Paul Weaver, perhaps there was no more greater moment of grace and completion than that of Brad and Susan Zimmerman at the Inman Park Trolley Barn (2003). Coworkers turned life partners, their engagement was a story of reclaiming peace and joy. Born on September 11, Susan understandably didn't feel like celebrating one bit on her birthday in 2001. As she watched the events unfold in New York City, she joined her boyfriend and the rest of the world in feeling depressed, shocked, and horrified. Susan's sense of national loss was deepened by what felt to be an attack on her personal mark of life itself. Birthdays are supposed to be safe harbors of happiness, not reminders of woe.

The emotional marring resurfaced when September rolled around again and Americans geared up for a difficult one-year anniversary. Here Brad and Susan faced a choice: would they celebrate, grieve, or do both? How were they supposed to unweave the ugly thread in time's great tapestry? Or was it a permanent insertion on the bartender's date of birth that hopefully would fade from memory if they just downplayed it long enough?

Brad Lee Zimmerman decided he wasn't about to let lunatics stain this wonderful day that had brought Susan into the world. He raised the relationship stakes and made a plan to propose marriage to her on her birthday. But this was no drink chalkboard cleverness. No, this would be an undertaking worthy of the Founding Fathers—popping the question while skydiving. The idea came to him late August during the middle of a business meeting. As Brad zoned out and pondered what was really important to him, the entire vision fell into to his mind like a stack of Lego blocks: proposal, birthday, skydiving, and a big sign on the ground asking for Susan's hand in marriage.

With a valiant plan of action, Brad got cooking on the details. He bought a ring from Brett at Decatur City Jewelers right off the Square and booked a trip with Skydive Atlanta in Thomaston, Georgia, for

September 11, 2002. He took it a step further and made it a double secret, telling everyone that Susan's surprise sign was to read, "Happy Birthday." Things were looking good in Brad's world except that he could not figure out how to make a sign large enough to see airborne. Like a procrastinating student with a term paper, Brad found himself sitting at the Pub's bar two days before launch at 9 P.M. with no sign and no leads to bring his brilliant idea to fruition. As panic began to engulf him, Brad cried to his coworker Brooke, who calmly suggested a roof tarp. Ah-ha! The crucial missing Lego locked into place and Brad tore off to Home Depot to give it a whirl.

The next morning saw Brad in his back yard with a 60' x 40' blue tarp, a gallon of white paint, a roller, and a mountain of doubt. Sure, he had correctly outlined the fourteen-foot letters, but what if you couldn't read the sign from way up high? What if Susan got terrified during the experience? What if he passed out on the way down and lost the ring? What if the whole idea just sucked? Brad ignored his inner peanut gallery and kept painting, feeling a tad bit alone with his secret. As he took a midday break, his roommate Paul Weaver came home and saw Brad's true intentions splattered in eggshell white. "Whatcha doing, Brad?" Paul inquired gleefully. The Brick Store bartender broke down and poured out fears that his cocksure proposal plan was actually cockamamie. It was less than twenty-four hours to liftoff and he hadn't a clue how that roof tarp was getting to Thomaston. Never fear, your friends are here.

As Brad let the cat out of the bag about proposing to Susan, the Pub kids rallied. Paul volunteered to make the hour's drive with the tarp, and Brooke and Ed agreed to ride shotgun under the pretense of supporting Susan on this important birthday. Many other coworkers decorated the bar with helium balloons later that evening and Kelley brought up her TV/VCR so they could watch the video replay. "Now get out of here and ask that girl to marry you!" With gratitude in his heart for this blessed workspace that to him represented a hotbed of humanity and a crucible of creative goodness, Brad streamed across town for a last minute haircut. Rose, his Vietnamese hairdresser, hugged him and smiled wide at the only words she understood, "Girlfriend. Marriage."

Susan never caught wind of Brad's scheme, as she was completely absorbed in the wonder of flying like an eagle and taking back her birthday and her country. It felt cleansing like American freedom itself. Little did she know that as the couple ascended 14,000 feet into the clear blue sky, a bright blue tarp was being unrolled at the landing site. Every employee of Skydive Atlanta was in on the fun. Whoever was not in the plane was standing on an edge of the tarp, including the next skydiving party. The experienced jumpers took Brad down first in a speed chute and kept Susan hanging for extra long airtime. As Susan fell ecstatically to the ground and the parachute popped at 5,000 feet, her tandem guide gave a shoulder tap and pointed down. Enormous white letters and an imperative came clear into view: "Marry Me Susan." Almost delirious, Susan tore off her jumpsuit and gave a breathy one-word affirmative answer. Rushing into an embrace, Susan's glazed eyes never left Brad's as he got down on one knee and slipped a ring onto her finger while the crowd roared. "The guy was a total ace. He plopped Susan right *on* the sign. Luckily she said yes," remembers Brad.

Hours before Brad and Susan Zimmerman's engagement at Skydive Atlanta

The exhausted couple went to celebrate the news with Susan's parents and then headed home to her apartment just a block away from the Square. Carefully Brad tucked the skydiving tape into his coat and greased the track for the last lap of his vision. "C'mon honey, let's go to the Pub for a nightcap. It's great we got engaged but it's your special day and we should celebrate that." Down Sycamore Road and up the alley they went, Susan catching a glimpse of the birthday balloons as she habitually peaked in the bar windows. Brad opened the doors to a packed house and Mike Gallagher stopped his entire restaurant to sing a tear-filled rendition of "Happy Birthday." As the new fiancés gathered their friends on the stairs so everyone could see the VCR player situated on the tee shirt cabinet, something magical happened. History rewrote itself as this intimate group watched very different events unfold on the screen. At least for them, the badly mangled thread became unraveled and rewoven with love and a promise of the future.

Brad and Susan got married a year later by Paul, who tenderly recounted the skydiving fairy tale with misty eyes. Their union symbolized many different patches on the Brick Store family quilt, particularly for Dave. Brad had first met his boss in a casual meeting in Athens over a sandwich counter with funnyman Sean Watkins (Brad and Paul's Decatur housemate). "Dave came in with a Frisbee and his trademark monkey grin throwing around a big 'Yeah man!' I liked him instantly." He followed Dave and Sean to the Mellow Mushroom and joined the kitchen staff and this band of pals. Years later when he started life anew, Brad intuitively revived his bond with the beer bar visionary. After leaving his drumming gig in rock band Dayroom, Brad drove straight to Decatur and landed on Dave and his wife Talia's front step like a lost puppy. The benevolent couple fostered Brad for three months until finding him a happy home with Paul, their minister-employee, through the Twains-Brick Store grapevine.

It was through this alliance that Paul observed his friend Brad mend a broken heart, fold into Decatur's scene, take root at the Pub, and gradually blossom into a loving partner for their mutual friend Susan. Now Paul had the honor of marrying the pair in front of so many whose hearts and hands had touched the Zimmerman circle over the years. There is a Chinese proverb that states, "One generation plants the trees. Another gets the shade." Dave Blanchard is a planter whose Brick Store tree shelters many.

What a privilege for the Decatur bar community to share this common thread of consecration with Paul, an individual whose steadfast, pure, and gentle demeanor welcomes all from either side of a bar. Paul sincerely appreciates the long standing relationships he has with the owners and staff of Twain's and Brick Store Pub, as well as the deep friendships he's forged with countless community members working and living in one of the southeast's Elysian Fields.

In a noisy, hectic bar situation, your best leader is someone who leads through the eyes alone. Paul has such ability. This internal presence also makes for the kind of man you want presiding over the most important day of your life. Considering Paul's own reverence for the institution of marriage, his active contribution to Decatur's common vision, and his high regard for the entrepreneurs, poets, artists, and madmen and women of the city, it is little wonder why he's in such demand among Brick Store wedding couples.

When Work Becomes Play: Brick Store Regulars

Australian writer Henry Lawson once said, "Beer makes you feel the way you ought to feel without beer." That's a dandy statement, and mostly true. A nice beer buzz can produce feelings of giddiness, the fall of defenses, statements of raw honesty, and group hugs, gosh darn it. Beer is downright terrific!

The caveat is the dark side of bar culture when a drinking establishment becomes a repository of negative energy. It's as if the stagnation is drenched into the walls and the barstools. Commiseration of sad times is an understandable affair to gather for drinks, as is the need to vent about bad breakups, crazy coworkers, and other life stressors. It's another matter completely when those gatherings stretch into weeks, months, and years, and your company is frequently just the bartender.

What's remarkable about the Brick Store clientele is that by and large no one looks to a "starter drink" to loosen them up, numb them out, or get them on the road to happy. Life itself is stimulant enough and folks come to relate and appreciate good beer and good friends. The Pub's dominant mood is positive because that is the prevailing attitude of the owners. The adage "you are the company you keep" says it all. At the Brick Store, it's a safe to say that the regulars are a positive addition to the ever-growing family of friends.

One such regular is Mark Sandlin, a graphic designer and bar patron since 1998. Living three miles due north of the Old Courthouse ("the mule knows the way"), Mark sums up his bi-weekly Brick Store pilgrimages like this: "Everyone brings something to the picnic, and it's a *great* picnic." From the onset Mark saw how everyone at the Pub was running in the same direction to make the place grand. It was this enthusiasm that attracted him over and over to sit for a spell at the bar and contribute his own picnic item: passion for his gifts. Mark resonated with the guys' authentic pursuit of happiness versus a mad, blind dash to some far-off business pinnacle. He himself had scaled down his medium-sized graphic design firm to a one-man show when Mark realized corporate management did not bring him joy. While there's something to be said about reaching for the brass ring, it's quite meaningful to Mark that the Pub's expression of greatness comes through simple things, such as a caring staff, a comfortable bar stool, and the humble offering of nature's finest ingredients.

William Carpenter, Ph.D., lead architect of the award-winning Lightroom Studio, finds Decatur and the Brick Store community a vortex of creatively supportive people. Throughout the late '80s, his North McDonough Road office was surrounded by boarded up buildings, yet Bill maintained a positive vision. So when this audacious alehouse opened up shop on the Square declaring itself a pub with a mission to establish a new world order of American bar culture, Bill was unfazed by the naysayers. He jumped right on the guys' wavelength and streamed through the doors with other likeminded souls. The architect's professional vision matched the Brick Store's almost point for point: fresh design solutions reached through the spirit of creativity and collaboration.

While living in the United Kingdom, Bill absorbed himself into the daily cycle enjoyed by the Brits—home, office, pub, home again. As such, it became a part of Bill's routine to finish drawing and walk up street to join his peers for a fellowship pint at the Brick Store. "This place has been a part of my being to the point where life and work has become the same thing. And that allows me to *play*. It's the greatest thing in life when you can't distinguish between work and play." Bill knows this intimately through his client-best friend relationships with Shawn Vinson and Will Draper, D.V.M., of Village Vets (aka Dr. Doolittle), with whom he connects over a beer as often as possible to discuss art, design, travel, and anything else under the sun.

There's no question that Dr. Will Draper loves the Pub—he holds the record for largest tab in a single night, $864 (even after a complementary discount), and yes, that bill is taped on his fridge. However, it's never about the imbibing alone. For Will, it's about being in an environment where he can flux from "secret society guy conversation," to date-night with the wife, to causal talk with his clients, to flying solo at bartender Steve's Belgian Bar (discussion topic: having their ashes spread at the Pub versus being placed in a German stein). "I could go into Dairy Queen and order a cup of water, and if they had the same staff attitude as here, I'd feel the same," Will sincerely exaggerates.

Then came Will's day of reckoning when his biological clock turned forty and he decided to make better friends with his local gym equipment. Although it pained him, the veterinarian fine ale drinker downshifted from twice-a-week to "semi-regular" visits (once every couple of weeks). Gracious as he is gifted, Will went out with a bang of gratitude and bought every single Brick Store Pub employee a $15 gift certificate from Decatur CD. "They are just a fabulous bunch of staff, many of them clients, too, and when I made the choice to become a less frequent face, I wanted to give them a parting token of my appreciation. I felt compelled to be the opposite of the type of customer who thinks it's okay to treat a server poorly."

Brick Store University

Another group of professionals who feel quite grateful for a place that meets the Brick Store's high standards is the academic set at Emory University, which is located just a few miles down the road from the Square. Professors and graduate students feel uplifted by the atmosphere created by a management that obviously strives for excellence, just as they do in their respected fields. There's also a decent stream of undergrads who seek a better option than pitchers of light beer and wings. If there's one thing an academic can do, that's discuss and debate. One such teacher brought his Greek and Roman history students to the Pub for an oratorical outing because he found it to be the closest thing he had to a symposium. The young professor found it a harsh reality when he moved away from the Decatur area and was hard pressed to find conversation-geared third places elsewhere. Now transplanted to Orlando, he cries for his old hangout.

When Emory School of Medicine opened the volunteer-centered Hope Clinic in April 2002 just two blocks from the Decatur Square, it was a major accomplishment for the university. As the first center of its kind in the nation, a state-of-the-art facility dedicated entirely to AIDS research and developing HIV vaccinations, the Hope Clinic stood for lofty ideals to help society. That's a mighty tall order, and the Brick Store was glad to do its part by fueling the brilliant crew several lunches a week with burgers, chips, and red pepper aioli (and rounds of beers on Fridays).

In its early years, the Hope Clinic was like any new large undertaking—wild, wooly, and a mound of effort. Sometimes the road felt bumpy and seemed dark, and so the Pub became a warm, familiar, welcomed escape on lunch hours. This Brick Store posse got rounded up almost daily by Hope Clinic manager Cathy Keeler, Decatur resident and fifth generation Atlantan of the Kirkwood family tree. As Cathy threw her heart into securing multi-million dollar grants, Karen Chan, R.N., contributed her researching skills to finding an HIV vaccine. "Not only did I make meaningful relationships with our Hope volunteers, but also lifetime friendships with colleagues, frequently over the best burgers in town," Karen remembers fondly.

Gerald Shadel, Ph.D., thought about submitting a meal ticket in his tenure package when he moved from Emory University to Yale University. A biochemistry professor for seven years through the Brick Store's early years, he frequented the Pub both socially and professionally, including a well-deserved and indulgent scotch session after defending his thesis. One late evening he, his wife, and several colleagues landed in a booth for an after-dinner drink following the Thrashers hockey game, when a server delivered him a shot of Wild Turkey with a note. "That ought to get your reactive oxygen species going, Dr. Shadel!" It was signed his "M1 Posse," which is shorthand for a first-year medical student. Gerald had just lectured on the medical condition of oxidative stress, which can be worsened by drinking straight Kentucky bourbon whiskey. The good natured scholar accepted the gift and later quipped,

"This would have been one of my most memorable nights at the Brick Store—if it weren't for that shot!"

Letting Down Your Hair

If the preceding scenario seems out of kilter—what is a university professional doing letting his hair down at a bar? —then you've never been to a place like the Brick Store. For if you had, you'd understand that a public house like this beckons to a broad cross section of the community. You might find regular Nick Purdy and his four children (all under the age of eight at the time of this storytelling) sitting on barstools with the help of Mom and Dad. Co-founder of *Paste* and a "solid Christian father," Nick unabashedly loves the Pub for its extraordinary feeling of intimacy and owner operating philosophy: every person is welcomed like a "guest in their home."

Still, isn't it unusual to have rug rats literally at the bar? Well, Nick folds his work and family time seamlessly into the Pub whenever possible. His sweet spot for meetings is what he calls the "four o'clock beer," which allows him to stay productive at the end of the workday while starting his evening a little early. He'd just finished one of those meetings when his wife Jenn called and told her husband to stay put—the family would come to Nick for dinner.

"I was still at the bar when they arrived, so Jenn and the kids joined me," recalls Nick of the rare occurrence. His wonderment with the Brick Store is the realization that in no other bar would both he and the bar staff feel okay about his children sitting at the counter. Nick corrects himself that this is not a bar, it's a *pub*. "There's power in a name. People are comfortable bringing their families," the native Atlantan asserts.

Nick's choice as a media entrepreneur has him in touch with trends, yet the Pub transcends all things vogue for him. He believes the guys are in the forefront of what's "post-cool," meaning people caring about what's real over what's hot. "When I am there, I feel comfortable and relaxed, as much as I can let my hair down in my own living room."

When his important guests are in town, Nick skips the fancy restaurants and opts instead for the genuine warmth of his unique local watering hole. His visitors quickly grasp that the Brick Store is so much more than great beer. For many of them, whose communities lack a third-place environment, the human touch of a tableside chat with the owner heightens their buzz above and beyond a premium drinking session. Their appreciation is evidenced by the mothers of Nick's friends asking to be brought back to the Pub even though they don't like beer. "There's a way that Dave, Mike, and Tom run this place that makes you feel cared for, respected, and yes, even loved, when you're in here," says Nick.

A founding member of All Souls Fellowship, Nick finds the Brick Store has more in common with a church than most would imagine. Both places satisfy a hunger to be known and accepted and a thirst for connection. Nick, like many others, sees a convivial pub as 100 percent necessary to a thriving, bonded community. "Wine makes glad the heart," as the Bible states (Psalm 104:15).

Thus, Nick and his fellow Christians come to the Decatur beer institution not to get drunk, but to do what everyone else is doing, namely getting out of the cares of the world and relate to each other in a place their families can enjoy. One of his fondest memories is the sight of thirty-five Presbyterian preachers out on the Pub's sidewalk, pints in hand, gathering for an area general assembly. "God is honored by excellence, so why would you drink crap beer?"

"God has a brown voice, as soft and full as beer."

—Anne Sexton, Pulitzer Prize winning poet

Soup of the Day: Thoughtfulness

Many dining establishments want to develop a friendly and familiar relationship with their clientele. Yet the hurried pace of a restaurant can quickly edge out this aspiration. It's even happening at the Pub where their immense popularity has shortened the staff's leisure time with the guests. So many friendly hands tug on the apron strings, and there's only so much time. That fact notwithstanding, the staff works miracles to squeeze in homey conversations at each table, especially if a customer is a pleasant regular.

Take long-time patron Cherie Kools, who spent the better part of the Pub's first ten years sharing lots of lunches and dinners of Brunswick stew and fish and chips with a group of her downtown Decatur coworkers. Birthdays, anniversaries, wedding showers, and bittersweet farewells—if there was any reason to go to the Brick Store, they went. Cherie felt like one of the Pub's number one fans even though she didn't drink beer. The staff certainly treated her like one of the family. In fact, Ryan Gallagher would have her sweet tea ready for her on the table before she even sat down, always "just the way I like it, with *lots* of ice."

As time went on, Cherie acquired a "bizarre and insatiable desire" for the Hungarian goulash special and started calling the Pub daily at 11:30 to ask for the soup of the day. One of the bar managers eventually noticed this pattern and responded to her, "Is this Cherie?" The staff member proceeded to take down her number on a post-it note and began leaving gleeful messages on her work voicemail that said, "Guess what soup we have today, my dear?"

There are plain Jane eateries, and then there are oases like the Brick Store. As Cherie puts it, "I can honestly say there's no other place where I've ever experienced such special attention and stellar treatment."

Your Drinks Are on Us

Roslyn and Mark Breitenbach had their first Brick Store experience the day they moved into their new Decatur home in 1999. After spending ten hours unpacking their belongings, the couple felt like anyone would moving in the June humidity: hot, sweaty, sticky, and hungry. When a neighbor came over to welcome them to the neighborhood, they asked where they should go to grab a quick bite of dinner. Rosalyn specifically asked for a place that wouldn't mind if they came in ratty shorts and tee shirts. The couple received directions to the obvious choice of the Brick Store and so they made their way to the Square.

The Breitenbachs immediately felt at ease in the Pub's atmosphere and shared their new resident status with the waitress. A few minutes later, an owner came out to their table and casually introduced himself. "Dave asked us where we had moved from and what brought us to town. After a very enjoyable conversation he said, 'Welcome to Decatur. Your drinks are on us.'" The couple couldn't get over this generous, hospitable gesture to two new members of the community. That night the Brick Store became their favorite restaurant and it has remained so to this day. Out-of-town guests automatically get taken to the comfort of the Pub, where Rosalyn and Mark enjoy retelling stories of the grateful day they adopted themselves into the Brick Store family.

Pub patron Jessica Rosenzweig didn't realize how lucky she was to have this gem so close to home until she moved away to Israel in August 2008. Jessica was living in Atlanta when she first completed a *Love at the Pub* survey, and a year later she wrote in again to fondly express her appreciation for everyone who makes the Brick Store Pub the place it is:

> *My last stop leaving for Israel was the Pub, and on my first trip back to the States I made sure to have a ten hour layover in Atlanta so I'd have the time to visit the Pub again. My friends knew that if I was having a bad day, I was at the Pub to cheer up, and if I was having a good day, I was at the Pub to celebrate. Throughout all my travels, be it Boston, NY, Miami, any place in between, or here in Israel, no venue has ever come close to being the home that the Pub was. With good beer, great staff, and the perfect atmosphere, no venue has compared. I am looking forward to the book so I can take a little bit of the Pub with me wherever I am. Thank you for all your hard work.*

Liquid Jesus

Certain other regulars had no clue what they'd just discovered until a sip of beer heaven woke them up to their surroundings. For this exercise, pretend you are a Midwestern man living in Chicago, who's just graduated from theology school and is about to interview at a little unknown Christian startup church in the Deep South. You bombed your last interview because the preacher's panel asked if you condone drinking (the answer of which you artfully and truthfully softened). Now you're on a plane accompanied by your wife and third child to Decatur, Georgia, a town of which you've never heard. Even though the head pastor sounds young and cool on the phone, you're not quite sure how to assuage a stereotypical knee-jerk reaction to your impending arrival to the Bible Belt. With zero expectations of a slam-dunk interview, you get picked up at the airport by the pastor. This man proceeds to drive you and your family directly to the Brick Store Pub and orders you an Aventinus Eisbock on draught.

Such is the true life history of Dan Adamson, assistant pastor at All Souls Fellowship and avid fan of the Brick Store Pub. Dan's account of what happened next approaches the sublime. "I took one sip of the Aventinus and thought, 'I have to get hired here. Please hire me for this job!' I hadn't even seen the church, met anyone other than Shayne, and yet I knew I *needed* to be in Decatur near this pub. We took pictures of the three of us at the Pub, Taqueria del Sol, and the Decatur CD store and sent them home, we were that excited about living here."

> **Eisbock** (Aventinus Weizen-Eisbock): are created by freezing off a portion of the water and removing it from the beer. This form of concentration increases the beer's body, flavor, and alcohol content. They can range from near black to as light as tawny red. Hop bitterness and flavor are mostly cast aside and replaced by the presence of big alcohol flavors, which can range from sweet to spicy, and fruity to fusel. Look for a heavy or almost syrupy body with tons of malty flavor.

Four years later, the assistant pastor looks quite at home in his comfortable, low-lit office. The walls display his children's art, while the clean-lined, black bookcase sports a Brick Store bumper sticker. There's even a faint pipe smell. Evidence of Dan's own fellowship at the Pub is found on his framed degree from St. Louis Covenant Theological Seminary, which is now plastered with a label for the Belgian beer Gulden Draak. "That is my new favorite beer, the one that replaced the Eisbock. It is so good, comes in that pretty white bottle . . . It's liquid Jesus." A Belgian strong dark ale weighing in at 11.2 ounces with 10.5 percent alcohol content, the Gulden Draak sounds like it might make one sink rather than walk on water.

When pressed for an explanation, Dan playfully insists that it was he and not his boss, Pastor Shayne, who first came up with the term "liquid Jesus." An easy joke would be, "It'll make you pray right over the commode," however these fathers and men of the cloth appreciate craftsmanship from an elevated perspective that most others don't. Dan and Shayne see beyond the holy works of Christian monks housed in the Brick Store, instead responding to what they consider the highest of all expressions, the human condition. To illustrate this point, here is insight by Bruce Larson and Keith Miller from Charles R. Swindoll's book *David: Man of Passion and Destiny* (Thomas Nelson, 1997):

> *The neighborhood bar is . . . permissive, accepting, and inclusive of fellowship . . . You can tell people secrets and they usually don't tell others or even want to. The bar flourishes not because most people are alcoholics, but because God has put into the human heart the desire to know and be known, to love and be loved.*

Bend It Like Brick Store: World Cup and BSFC

To state the obvious, it's really cool to own your own bar: your place, your rules. So if you're going to break a cardinal rule in your own establishment—like no TVs in the Brick Store Pub—break it with class and style. That's exactly what Dave, Mike, and Tom did when they installed two giant flat screen televisions in their hallowed Belgian Bar to show every soccer match of the 2006 World Cup. Hosted in Germany from June through July, this once-every-four-years international event represents the best of the best in a sport considered the world's game. What a perfect metaphor for the world class beer served in the European setting of America's third leading pub.

The news of this perfect anomaly spread quickly across metro Atlanta's soccer community. "TVs in the Brick Store? Wait, they're showing the *World Cup*? That's awesome. When are we going?" It was as if Gotham City's Bat Signal was shining above the Belgian Bar calling for an elevated standard of guy culture to come watch this highly anticipated football contest. Men will attest that watching a great game with your mates is sacred time: no fanfare, not a lot of talk, just some good food, cold brews, the tube, your friends, and it's a beautiful party. But how was one supposed to revel in male bonding when the matches started so early in the morning and ran four weeks solid? Sure, you could watch USA versus Czech Republic on Monday morning at 8 A.M. by yourself with your dog and some coffee. Or you could go to the Pub and join sixty other rabid fans where the action of the

Nuremburg stadium felt up close and personal. Here you could cocoon under the low rafter ceiling of the Belgian Bar with authentic German pub signage, black Guinness pints, orange Weihenstephaners, and bratwurst sandwiches. A "sick day" was in order.

Two games were played every day from early morning through lunchtime. Nary a soul came for the beginning round games, save for the USA matches. However, during the quarterfinals, semifinals, and the final matches the bar was crammed elbow-to-elbow. You would be lucky to have a clear view of the teams let alone a seat or even a spot on the floor. That made it all the more fun, especially when high-fives exploded all around you, strangers becoming friends in a matter of minutes. Super-long lunches got scheduled, and some patrons even brought their bosses. Many others gathered friends from all over town. It didn't matter if you came by yourself, as there were always folks you knew. From Pub standards to Atlanta's international community, the same faces appeared day after day to root for the thirty-plus qualifying world teams.

"Some people think football is a matter of life and death. I assure you, it's much more serious than that."

—Bill Shankly, legendary U.K. soccer player and manager

There was such specialness about the whole tournament. Brick Store regulars and staff alike soaked in the quiet, pristine beauty of the Belgian Bar and the rarity of a television set. Hardly anyone outside of management was accustomed to being up in this space during the early part of the day when the room dispensed sunlight like grace through the skylight. You would have thought you had entered a chapel. Then at night, once last call was made and the regular clientele went home, employees would indulge themselves with late-night movie sessions. It felt like Christmas in July as staff snuggled up with De Dolle Ara Beir and bartender Gentleman Jesse's collection of Hugh Grant movies. Such is privilege.

Then there was the legion of Brick Store soccer fans that were pinching themselves because it was finally World Cup time again *and* they were watching it in forbidden paradise. "It was like parents had lifted curfew for a few weeks," gushed one grown father of two. For years, soccer geeks had begged Dave to "please, please, please" put TVs in the Pub just for soccer to no avail. The guys' commitment to customer satisfaction is etched in stone and no special request is considered worth disrupting the normal flow of their restaurant. The trio of Pub owners even turned down legendary singer Tom Wait's request to reserve the Belgian Bar for a party after his Atlanta tour show (a slightly big deal given Mike and Dave's reverence for musicians). But of course, granting such a wish would have excluded their regular patrons.

This international football engagement was different. If there was ever an event worth bending the rules, the 2006 World Cup was it. First, the matches were finished long before the space opened in late afternoon. So the guys could pull off something like TVs and a sports crowd and not show up their regular business. Second, it just made sense. Here was the universality of beer and soccer coming together under one roof and uniting in the highest order. Finally, Dave's goalie heart bled passionately for that tiny white soccer bar whizzing across the field. He watched every single match, sometimes all by his lonesome, giving his ESPN-worthy analysis of the U.S. team's disappointing show to anyone who would listen.

"World Cup is the best sporting event in the world. I love its spirit, history, and non-commercialization," said Dave. Spoken like a man devoted to promoting the rich tradition of brewing and drinking high quality beer in a stripped down fashion that is so honored in European pub culture. The folks "across the pond" get pretty excited about their "football," and for those four weeks watching the tournament in the Belgian Bar it was easy to understand the fanaticism. When the bar crowd swelled to 150 people for the big matches, the excitement was contagious and intense. As Italy progressed to an ultimate cup victory, the small soccer community felt satisfied and full from drinking their own cup of world class football.

Bittersweet for many, the TVs got yanked off the walls the second the final clip was played. The reality set in that it would be another long four years before the next fix.

Dave Blanchard walks his talk when it comes to soccer, as evidenced by the Brick Store Football Club (BSFC), a team on which he plays goalie. BSFC is a group of guys in their 30s and a few in their early 40s who get together every Thursday to play a little soccer. Many are married. Many have kids. All have their best playing days behind them. But they all love playing soccer, drinking beer, and doing these things together whenever possible, usually with the beer following the soccer but not always.

Don't look for BSFC on the cover of *Sports Illustrated*, but know that this small band of athletes has both a winning record and the best looking jerseys in the metro Atlanta league (Dave is as choosy about fashion as he is about beer). Bar sponsorship of local sports clubs is commonplace. Bar owners on your team, well, that's plain fun if for nothing else, the cool-by-association and fantasy factor of "If I could own a bar . . ."

For example, on a perfect spring night there is a gentle, warm breeze blowing through the open door and windows of the Brick Store. Everyone in town has broken out their favorite short-sleeved tee shirt and a feeling of childhood freedom permeates the air. Instead of freeze tag, the staff plays a made-up version of the "name game." Bartender Matt stomps down the Pub steps muttering loudly, "You can't pick your own nickname." Dave happens to be passing Matt on the way up to the office and pauses in curiosity of his Pub child's statement. Matt continues without missing a beat: "Jesse wants to call himself 'Smid'y'!" Dave holds a one-second manager/father's meeting and roars, "Yes!" with a high five and big toothy grin, as he scoots up the stairs.

This particular night is a Thursday and the majority of the BSFC has gathered along the Pub's long wooden bench for a team meeting. Dave is beaming as he returns to the table from his little errand, fetching a photo disk for a project on his nationally renowned bar, and gives this author a quick introduction: "Hey, guys, this is my friend who's writing the book on this place." It's a well-deserved moment for Dave to savor, a beautiful evening where he gets to actually sit down at his labor-of-love Pub and enjoy his staff and his two passionful hobbies—beer and soccer—as they meld. As much as this good-looking group of professionals love and appreciate their day jobs, a natural twinge of envy surfaces. Their corporate huddles certainly don't look like this (refer to Part One or Two for a reality check of bar ownership).

Dave is just like every other guy on his team, though, juggling the same balls of work-spouse-children-playtime. These Thursday nights together are a precious outlet and they make the most of them. First impressions of BSFC spoke volumes to lawyer Andrew Hall who joined the team after it had been well established. Andrew had been going to the Brick Store for a long time before joining BSFC and was well versed in the high-quality beers that they served. After his first BSFC match played at the Atlanta Silverbacks soccer arena, the group retired to Dave's pickup truck in the parking lot to partake of some beverages. Imagine Andrew's surprise when Dave opened up his cooler and he saw something you'd never find within the four walls of the Brick Store: a cold suitcase of Miller Genuine Draft in cans. His eyes popped. "Here I was with one of the owners of the Brick Store drinking MGD in a parking lot of the Silverbacks' Park. Deep inside, Dave has some beer can drinking 'skillz' [vital guy culture trait]. I was sold and, when healthy, have been a BSFC man ever since."

There is an ancient philosophical riddle that poses: Why do men do anything, really? To illustrate this point and why it's crucial for the male species to gather on their own far, far away from their wives, let's study the BSFC roster, in particular Dave Newman, soccer striker extraordinaire, who apparently can calculating the swing speed of a timber sports competitor and a major league baseball player relying on the ancient Greek concept of phi. To sum up this fellowship of the Pub, Andrew lends some wisdom:

> *Some weeks we win. We love winning. Some weeks we lose. We hate losing. It may be a hackneyed phrase, but win or lose we do things together as BSFC and, afterwards, we sit around drinking beer, from cans, and enjoy the remainder of our Thursday respite from our otherwise busy lives, drinking beer and sharing a little fellowship. And in some way, isn't that what the Brick Store is for all of us—sans the cans, of course.*

Our Daily Thanks: Staff Holidays

If you ask most servers how the Brick Store ranks as a restaurant industry job, there's an accordant reply: The Pub is the top of the food chain. With few exceptions, servers leave this job to pursue a life dream rather than to schlep dishes somewhere else. As described in Part One (Treat Your Staff with Consummate Respect), this all boils down to respect from the owners—respect for their servers as individuals and as a hard working team aiming to perform their jobs well every time.

Just imagine if your employer allowed a dress-down policy every day, if every schedule request was given serious consideration, if you could decide what music was played on the airwaves, if you were offered a low price on your beers on and off your shift, and if your work environment was organized for maximum efficiency and flow. Now imagine if your boss was someone you could approach openly about any job-related or personal problem, someone you could ask for advice, and someone you felt you could call under duress (for example, a car accident or needing to get bailed out of jail). Can you even comprehend your employers shutting down their lucrative business for the entire day and evening so that you and your coworkers could go and play?

Welcome to the refreshing reality of the Brick Store Pub, a workplace that feels like home. Dave, Mike, and Tom follow a simple and profound management philosophy, which is to treat others the way you want to be treated. Outstanding guest service starts and ends with the staff, so is it really any mystery that keeping the "kids" happy keeps everyone happy? "I know that if we make the staff come first, then it's automatic that our guests are taken care of properly," says Mike.

When you operate a bar, it's a given that you'll be open on or around all major holidays. Instead of swapping stories with Grandma, you're bringing someone else's granny sweet tea and a pint of cider. Empathy for their employees prompted Dave to suggest they close down for the afternoon before Thanksgiving that first year in 1997 to host a staff holiday complete with a turkey dinner. The guys put a "closed for lunch" note on the door that Wednesday, lined up the tables in a banquet style, provided an open bar, and cooked a big bird for everyone to enjoy. Perhaps Tom spilled too much Jamison into the gravy tray, however the love flowing from that kitchen and onto the dinner table wrapped an invisible hug around every single person there.

Pub Staff Thanksgiving table

Mike's reaction to his partner's suggestion captures the nature of love at the Pub. "A staff holiday . . . that's obviously a great idea." As Mike recalls, it was not a matter of owing anything to the staff, rather knowing they had created something special in their business and that they wanted to treat their employees like a family. A big feast made complete sense. For some, it's the only Thanksgiving meal they'll have. For many industry veterans, it's the first experience of an owner bothering to care.

Kourtney had been waiting tables for a little over two months when Brick Store Thanksgiving 2006 rolled around. As she took in the informal gathering with a pint of Guinness, she already knew that she loved the Pub and would be working there for a long time. It took her no time at all to recognize the strength of the triad. "Mike does the toasts, Dave is anal about the way things look, and Tom keeps it running like a ship."

As the child of deli-owning parents, Kourtney appreciates working hard for independent proprietors who don't think twice about assisting her during the dinner rush. In her mind, the Pub stood head and shoulders above the rest of her wait jobs thanks to this authentic "got your back" attitude and the complementary personalities and signature presence of the three owners. "The guys all are so different and they each bring a part of themselves to make the restaurant what it is. I feel like I'm an extension of that family, and so I strive to take the guys' essence and bring it out on the floor." Coming from an extensive corporate restaurant background where it's easy to feel like a number, Kourtney felt impressed with the high level of trust emanating from Dave, Mike, and Tom. This show of turkey good will sealed the deal, bumping up her bosses' opinion another ten notches.

Brick Store staff Thanksgiving is now a decade-old institution that has changed little even though the family has grown exponentially. Every year the cooks get kicked out of the kitchen so Tom and Mike can enjoy the privilege of basting, baking, and frying whatever's not nailed down to the counter. Coworkers old and new saddle in with side dishes like their mom used to make (or a heaping plate of supermarket hot wings if they are too hung over to cook). It's all on the table: free range turkey, vegan mashed potatoes, green beans in ham hocks, Tofurkey, wild rice, pumpkin pie, store-bought cupcakes, beer, whiskey, dignity, respect, and love. "Even if only two staff members come to this dinner, it's worth it," shares Mike.

"For me, it's beyond being worth it," he continues. "I love it. I look forward to it every year as much as I do Thanksgiving with my own family. It's rare that I get a chance to sit down with them [staff] to eat a meal and share a conversation." To Mike, the meaning of gratitude is seeing everyone sitting down, enjoying a great dinner, and relaxing.

Sometimes it seems like yesterday that the Brick Store opened with ten employees (swiftly growing to seventeen the first year). Whereas they used to have one server working on Saturdays, it now it takes seventeen staff members to run the place on a Friday night alone. The Pub is busy nearly every night of the week. Weekends see it jammed from the back wall of the second floor Belgian Bar all the way out into the street.

Lugging heavy trays of Abbey ale all over a crowded restaurant for eight to ten hours is backbreaking work for servers. By the end of the night, they're exhausted and glad when things wind down. Although it's a great overall feeling, it can be downright tuckering to host a huge party night after night. Burnout is normal, and rejuvenation is a must. Dave, Mike, and Tom's solution: Big Day Out and Big Night In.

Big Day Out is another Brick Store institution that began as a matter-of-fact statement from the mouth of Tom Moore in early May 1998. On a picture-perfect afternoon, Tom emerged from the windowless kitchen and stepped outside into the spring air. "No one should have to work on a pretty day like this," he said. Just like that, the guys closed down the Pub the following Monday and took the whole crew over to Lake Claire Park for softball, Frisbee, and cold Warsteiner. It was a welcome break for the entrepreneurs, and an instant hit for the staff whose morale already was sky high.

How could you not like working in this homegrown little pub with its plethora of cool regulars, eclectic beer, and young bosses who would openly giggle with you about stuff like music, hairdos, clothes, sports, pop culture, and everything else? *And now you're giving us the day off and taking us to play softball? Count me in!*

Everyone met at the Pub around eleven o'clock and started drinking Bloody Marys. Suntan lotion was applied amidst pre-softball eats of Sweet Melissa's pancakes, biscuits, and coffee. Cooks and servers enjoyed some laidback bonding time while Dave, Mike, and Tom relished the fact that it was their place and they could close it any day they wanted. Like that day, a perfect spring outing. Someone playfully called out, "Hey, watch out, y'all, it's Brick Store's big day out!" Water coolers were filled and off the staff went to nurture their inner children's need for romping and stomping.

A healthy number of players were self-proclaimed non-jocks, so most of their day was filled with cracking jokes to ease low-level batting anxiety. Well, that and shouting sarcastic funnies from the woods, as there was no bathroom and no one had remembered to bring toilet paper. They became the cheerleaders for the boys and girls whose athleticism did sizzle and shine.

Pub Bartender Shannon Barnes gets greased up for Big Day Out

Although no one gave the Atlanta Braves a run for their money, there was a home run moment that would have gained Chipper Jones' nod of approval. As cook Blake Guthrie pulled up late to the park, he heard his name being screamed as next up in the batting order. He stumbled quickly down the steep, kudzu-encrusted hill and straight to home plate where someone handed him a bat. Blake looked up and saw a softball hurtling toward him, so he hit it. The ball sailed back to the tennis courts and Blake ran all four bases back to home plate where someone else handed him a beer. He chugged his victory cup and went immediately over to the keg for another as the entire group cheered. "You know this moment is going down in history," Dave Blanchard stated.

It was good, clean fun until the keg kicked, the smokes ran out, and everyone wanted to leave the park. After laughing hard all day at each other's heroics and bloopers, no one wanted the party to end. So the softball crowd picked up and took their sunburns over to the "Ridley House," a nearby home where three staff members lived, including Tom's future wife Melissa. Here the silly togetherness vibe continued with the added bonus of a pool. As the evening wrapped up with impromptu guitar jams and cannon ball dives off the roof, the guys sat back in their pool chairs with a satisfied feeling of watching their children play.

Big Day Out, always held on a Monday, is the envy of the workers in the local restaurant industry scene who wish their bosses were as cool as Dave, Mike, and Tom. The event has barely changed since the first year, except for its growth from fourteen to forty people (and moving to a new field location that has bathrooms). A camaraderie cornerstone, the Pub kids look forward to this employee holiday *almost* as much as the owners. "Staff parties bring out the child inside each of us. Parties are fun, so we have them, and don't take things too seriously," says Tom with simple wisdom. Clear evidence of this philosophy is Big Night In, the sister evening event to Big Day Out, which replaced the Ridley House pool parties.

Held at the Brick Store, Big Night In keeps the carousing safely contained (the guys hire a late night limousine to get everyone home). More importantly, it satisfies a hunger to ditch the bar rags and get dolled up for each other as Big Night In is a themed formal festivity. Past fetes include County Western, Mexican Riviera, Casino, and '80's Prom (complete with a photographer for prom pictures). The guys roll out the red carpet as usual by providing an open bar and a buffet, and hiring outside bartenders from other Decatur establishments. Some years an ice sculpture appears on the front table, cleverly designed so party guests can do Jägermeister shots in an Olympic-style luge track (this liquor run ain't pretty, but it's pretty fun). Clean up the next day usually lasts through lunchtime, as do the hangovers.

Although Brick Store holidays are the ultimate reset button for his staff, there's one bummer for Dave: the possibility of letting down a patron who made a special trip to the Brick Store that same day. The possibility of disappointing someone is a chance he has to take, however, for the sanity, health, and morale of his extended family.

For Tom, it's crystal clear why they go through the effort of staff parties: "The biggest complaint of any employee is the feeling of being used like an asset rather than treated as a person. This is all about showing respect for our employees and engendering loyalty, trust, and a feeling of care."

As a fitting end to this tale, sweetly imagine little Davey Blanchard playing fort high up in a tree. Suddenly, he hears the unmistakable sound of a bell, his mother's family dinner bell announcing that it was time to come home to the supper table. This very same bell now sits atop the Pub's roof. Although rarely used and almost unnoticeable, it is perhaps the most binding symbol of love at the Pub. To illustrate, imagine once more that it is thirty years later and that another young man is playing high in a tree. This time it is Pub cook Sean Grapevine who had wandered outside during the ten year staff reunion party and boyishly climbed thirty feet up a holly tree on the Square. Someone whistled for Sean to "come get down out of that tree and get inside," as it was time for the big toast. Children at heart, Dave, Mike, and Tom thankfully are always calling their extended family home to the supper table.

As always, thank you, Brick Store Pub.

Epilogue

Hot Diggity Dog—Let's Go to the Pub!

Well, it's time for "last call." You don't have to stop reading, but the storytelling has got to end here. By now you've drunk your fill (and then some) of what makes the Brick Store Pub a top-ranked beer-drinking establishment: outstanding craftsmanship, dedication to conversation, and a love of community that bursts at its seams. In our hearts the Brick Store is more than a national star, a cultural treasure, or the epitome of the American Dream. It's a significant third place we consider home. And it doesn't get any better than that.

What's that? You want just one more story? Aw, what the heck. Well, we'd love to tell you about server Megan Allinger and Pub regular Craig Beezley—how their tableside conversation about a mutual love for the "Great Outdoors" led to a trip together out West and a subsequent engagement ring—but their tale has barely gotten started. Here's a quick one for the road that's sure to bring a smile…

It was the opening series of the Atlanta Braves and word got around the Pub that a group outing was forming for staff, close friends of the owners, and baseball fanatics. Game Day arrived and a cast of twenty folks shuffled into the Brick Store just about half past five. An instant tailgate formed around the downstairs bar, as pre-game Terrapin Pale Ales, Victory Prima Pilsners, and pretzel appetizers went down everybody's hatch.

Meanwhile, there was some kind of fuss happening down the hall by the kitchen window. You could feel it clear at the top of the bar. One by one the ball crowd felt themselves being pulled past the server station and toward the bathrooms to see what was causing the hubbub.

It was there, just past the ice container with a clear view of the kitchen grill, that the touching answer revealed itself.

Here was Michael Gallagher making over sixty hot dogs for the Braves game. The Irishman had his grill covered end to end with crowd-pleasing wieners and was focused like a laser beam on his task. Never mind that it was the beginning of the restaurant's dinner hour and food tickets were coming into the window, this was baseball tradition and the host had a hungry flock to feed.

Presto, Mike hustled the frankfurters into cellophane wrap and pointed everyone out the door to the MARTA train. The pleasantly buzzed group piled on public transit and down to the stadium, resisting the urge to sneak a bite of the goodies. The wafting smell of baseball franks was driving everyone crazy in a good way. As the Decatur crew finally settled into their nosebleed seats, hot dogs sailed down the aisles like a Georgia miracle. By the third inning, every single person munched in bliss, sipped beer, and giggled, as dogs got tossed seven rows down. It was a shame the Braves lost. However, Mike's loving intention made it feel like a grand slam evening.

The fable of the Pub relates that three rainbows were seen near the area the day the Brick Store opened. It's easy to imagine that as true, as there is no end to this love story. It goes on forever. As one former longtime bartender states, "I wish I could make it mandatory for everyone in the world to work like this." With so many lives touched and enhanced by the Pub—by all of the Decatur community, really—it's safe to say that this living, breathing tale is an open book. So why not go down to the Brick Store and create (or expand) your own chapter.

Thanks, and we'll see you at the Pub.

"May your glass be ever full. May the roof
over your head be always strong. And may
you be in heaven half an hour before the devil
knows you're dead."

—Old Irish Toast

Love Is by Michael Gallagher

Love is never having to drink beer made with rice and corn.

True love is that first sip of a perfectly poured pint of Guinness.

Love is a medium rare burger topped with blue cheese, bacon and mushrooms.

Love is lettuce lovingly pulled out of the ground yesterday morning.

Love is when you're talking over lunch, look down, and realize the side of red pepper aioli you just asked for is already on the table.

Love is the server who runs after you to give you the cell phone left on the table.

Love is the host at the restaurant who offers you a towel because you just ran in from the pouring rain.

Love is your coworker scrubbing the fryer pans, for you—which are hot and black and greasy—and never saying a word about it.

Love is a corned beef sandwich where the beef is cooked to a slight crisp, succulent perfection and the bread grilled to where it just begins to brown and it arrives at the table still sweating.

Love is that first dunk of your fish into a very special remoulade sauce and remembering how much you love fish and chips with a pint of locally brewed beer.

Love is your bartender remembering your face on only your second visit and welcoming you with a warm, genuine smile . . . a new home.

Love is the server who doesn't just take your order . . . they take care of you. They love their job.

Your Support Lives On

Thank you for supporting *Love at the Pub*. The art of life is being in the natural flow of giving and receiving. So in the spirit of giving back, we are grateful to donate a portion of the author proceeds to children's charities that benefit from SkaterAid.

SkaterAid. Founded in 2005, SkaterAid is an annual skateboard and music festival in Decatur, Georgia. Proceeds from SkaterAid are used to assist families of children who are dealing with pediatric cancer. The festival provides a space for teenagers to celebrate their youth through music and skateboard contests. The community is further united through a silent auction of skateboard decks decorated by local artists.

To learn more on the inspiration for SkaterAid, review Part Three, Life Happens in a Bar: The Birth of SkaterAid. For more information on the event, visit www.skateraid.net.

Resources

Note: With few exceptions, all resources listed here have been referenced in Love at the Pub. Many more city resources are found at www.decaturga.com. Author takes no responsibility for the continued accuracy of contact information.

Brick Store Pub
125 East Court Square
Decatur, Georgia 30030
(404) 687-0990
www.brickstorepub.com

Hours:
Monday: 11 A.M.–1 A.M.
Tuesday–Saturday: 11 A.M.– 2 A.M.
Sunday: 12 P.M.–1 A.M.

The Belgian Bar opens at:
5 P.M. Sunday–Thursday
4 P.M. Friday
12 P.M. Saturday

The kitchen stops serving one hour before closing time each night.

No reservations or requests for rentals or receptions are accepted. Groups of eight to ten are easily accommodated before 5:30 P.M. Monday through Thursday. A waiting list typically begins around 6 P.M. every day of the week. The Pub is not built to accommodate groups of twelve or more during busy times, so large parties are *strongly* encouraged to come early. There is plenty to drink while you wait!

City of Decatur

City of Decatur
www.decaturga.com

Decatur Arts Festival
www.decaturartsfestival.com

Decatur Book Festival
www.decaturbookfestival.com

Decatur Library
www.dekalblibrary.org

Great Decatur Beer Festival
www.decaturbeerfestival.com

Decatur Book Shops and Coffee Shops

Blue Elephant Book Shop
www.blueelephantbookshop.com
(404) 728-8955

Books Again
225 N. McDonough Rd, Decatur
(404) 377-1444

Dancing Goats Coffee Bar
www.dancinggoatscoffee.com
(404) 687-1100

Eagle Eye Book Shop
www.eagleeyebooks.com
(404) 486-0307

Javamonkey
www.javamonkeydecatur.com
(404) 378-5002

Little Shop of Stories
www.littleshopofstories.com
(404) 373-6300

Decatur Blogs and Literary Resources

Baby Got Books
www.babygotbooks.com

Bill Floyd Decatur
www.billfloyddecatur.com

Decatur Metro
http://decaturmetro.com

inDecatur
http://airbornecombatengineer.typepad.com/in_decatur/

Next Stop Decatur
http://next-stop-decatur-ga.blogspot.com

Decatur Schools and Universities

Agnes Scott College
www.agnesscott.edu
(404) 471-6000

City Schools of Decatur
www.decatur-city.k12.ga.us
(404) 370-4400

Emory University
www.emory.edu
(404) 727-612

Decatur Holistic Practices

Center for Holistic Health
www.centerforholistichealth.com
(404) 929-0604

Decatur Healing Arts
www.decaturhealingarts.com

Decatur Business Associations and Shopping Districts

Decatur Business Association
www.decaturdba.com
(404) 371-8386

East Decatur Station
www.eastdecaturstation.com
(404) 377-3095

Oakhurst Village
www.oakhurstga.org

Decatur Bars, Clubs, and Restaurants

Eddie's Attic
www.eddiesattic.com
(404) 377-4976

James Joyce Irish Pub
www.jamesjoyceirishpub.net
(404) 378-5097

Leon's Full Service
www.leonsfullservice.com
(404) 687-0500

Our Way Café
www.ourwaycafe.com
(404) 292-9356

Sweet Melissa's
www.sweetmelissas.com
(404) 370-1111

Twain's Billiards and Tap
www.twains.net
(404) 373-0063

Decatur and Atlanta Arts and Music

Amador Photo
www.amadorphoto.com

Blake Guthrie
www.blakeguthrie.com

Decatur CD
www.decaturcd.blogspot.com

DoucheMaster Records
www.myspace.com/douchemasterrecords

Eddie's Attic
www.eddiesattic.com
(404) 377-4976

Gentleman Jesse and His Men
www.myspace.com/gentlemanjesse

Kodac Harrison
www.kodacharrison.com

Loss Cat
www.losscat.com

Paste Magazine
www.pastemagazine.com

Pete the Cat
www.petethecat.com

Ruth Franklin
www.ruthfranklin.com

SkaterAid
www.skateraid.net

Stomp and Stammer
www.stompandstammer.com

Vinson Gallery
www.vinsongallery.com

Decatur Craftsmen, Architects, and Builders

Andrew Maslanka Creative Services
Maslanka_3@hotmail.com

Lightroom Studio
www.lightroom.tv
(404) 377-6889

Phillip Raines Restoration Mason
(404) 786-4904

Volkmar Wochatz, DBA Hausbau L.L.C., Carpenter
(404) 378-5504

Watershed Development
www.watersheddevelopment.com
(404) 373-3005

Decatur Banking and Real Estate

Decatur First Bank
www.decaturfirstbank.com
(404) 373-1000

Emilie Markert Real Estate
www.emiliemarkert.com
(404) 378-9300

Lance Deen Sanctuary Real Estate
www.lancedeen.com
(404) 502-4339

Decatur Shopping

Decatur City Jewelers
www.decaturcityjewelers.com
(404) 377-7643

Hoopla
www.hooplakids.com
(404) 371-9485

Seventeen Steps
(404) 377-7564

Squash Blossom Boutique
www.squashblossomboutique.com
(404) 373-1864

Stratosphere Skate Shop
www.stratosphereskateboards.com
(404) 521-3510

That Pottery Place
www.potteryplacedecatur.com
(404) 371-4557

Decatur Services

Lenz Marketing
www.lenzmarketing.com
(404) 373-2021

Neil's Restoration Classic Cars
(404) 292-9333

Rutabaga Salon
(404) 377-8900

Terra Mater Salon
www.terramatersalon.com
(404) 377-7039

Village Vets
www.thevillagevets.com
(404) 371-0111

Decatur and DeKalb Churches and Groups

All Souls Fellowship
www.allsoulsfellowship.org
(404) 270-9900

DeKalb Rape Crisis Center
www.dekalbrapecrisiscenter.org
(404) 377-1429
Crisis Hotline: (404) 377-1428

Oakhurst Recovery Program
www.oakhurstrecovery.com
(404) 371-0590

Veritas Church
www.veritaschurch.net
(404) 370-3977

YMCA of Metro Atlanta
www.ymcaatlanta.org

Government, Foundations, and Transportation

DeKalb History Center
www.dekalbhistory.org
(404) 373-1088

Emory University Hope Clinic
www.hopeclinic.emory.edu
(877) 424-HOPE

Georgia House Representative Stephanie Stuckey
www.stephaniestuckeybenfield.org
(404)656-7859

MARTA
www.itsmarta.com

PATH Foundation
www.pathfoundation.org

Zip Car
www.zipcar.com

Atlanta Resources

Atlanta Braves
http://atlanta.braves.mlb.com

Georgia Aquarium
www.georgiaaquarium.org
(404) 581-4000

Inn at Serenbe
www.serenbeinn.com
(770) 463-2610

Lakewood Antique Market
www.lakewoodantiques.com
(770) 889-3400

Le Moulin Rouge
www.parisonponce.com
(404) 249-9965

Skydive Atlanta
www.skydiveatlanta.com
(800) 276-DIVE

The Trolley Barn
www.thetrolleybarn.com
(404) 521-2308

Athens Resources

40 Watt Club
www.40watt.com
(706) 549-7871

Classic City Brew Fest
www.classicitybrewfest.com

The Globe
www.classiccitybrew.com/globe.html
(706) 353-4721

The Grit
www.thegrit.com
(706) 543-6592

The University of Georgia
www.uga.edu
(706) 542-3000

Georgia Beer Resources

5 Seasons Brewing
www.5seasonsbrewing.com
(770) 521-5551

Atlanta Brewing Company
www.atlantabrewing.com

Sweetwater Brewing Company
www.sweetwaterbrew.com
(404) 691-2537

Terrapin Beer Company
www.terrapinbeer.com
(706) 549-3377

National and International Beer Resources

Anchor Brewing Company (CA)
www.anchorbrewing.com

Dogfish Head Brewing and Eats (DE)
www.dogfish.com
(302) 226-2739

Ebenezer's Pub (ME)
www.ebenezerpub.net

Guinness (Ireland)
www.guinness.com

Monk's Cafe (PA)
www.monkscafe.com
(215) 545-7005

North Coast Brewing Tap Room and Brewery (CA)
www.northcoastbrewing.com
(707) 964-BREW

Oskar Blues Cajun Grill and Brewery (CO)
www.oskarblues.com
(303) 823-6685

Unibroue (Canada)
www.unibroue.com

Victory Brewing Company and Restaurant (PA)
www.victorybeer.com
(610) 873-0881

Belgium Beer Resources

Achel
www.achelsekluis.org

Chimay
www.chimay.com

Koningshoeven
www.koningshoeven.nl

Orval
www.orval.be

Rochefort
www.trappistes-rochefort.com

Westmalle
www.trappistwestmalle.be

Westvleteren
www.sintsixtus.be/eng/brouwerij.htm

Beer Publications and Associations

All About Beer Magazine
www.allaboutbeer.com

BeerAdvocate
www.beeradvocate.com

Brewers Association
www.beertown.org

RateBeer
www.ratebeer.com

Southern Brew News
www.brewingnews.com/southernbrew

World of Beer
http://worldofbeer.wordpress.com

Brick Store Pub Beer Distributors and Suppliers

B. United International
www.bunitedint.com

D&V International
www.specialtybeer.com

Georgia Crown Distributing Company
http://www.georgiacrown.com

Merchant du Vin
www.merchantduvin.com

Savannah Distributing Company
http://www.gawine.com

Bibliography

Beaumont, Stephen. *A Taste for Beer*. Darby, PA: Diane Publishing Company, 1995.

Oldenburg, Ray. *The Great Good Place: Cafes, Coffee Shops, Bookstores, Bars, Hair Salons, and Other Hangouts at the Heart of a Community*. New York, NY: Da Capo Press, 1999.

Swindoll, Charles. *David: Man of Passion and Destiny*. Nashville: Thomas Nelson, 2000.

About the Author

Mary Jane Mahan is an adventurous soul exploring life's path as the Chief Emotional Architect of MaryJaneBrain Productions. As a teenager, she wrote poems under the moon. Today she open heartedly expresses her creative gifts as an author, actor, and public speaker. *Love at the Pub* is her first book.

A native Philadelphian, Mary Jane took root in the South in 1994 after arriving to earn a masters degree in speech communication from the University of Georgia. She moved from Athens to Decatur, Georgia, in June 1997 and put her degree to work on the floor of the Brick Store Pub as the tenth hired employee. It was a grand way to spend eighteen months, full of wonder and love reminiscent of her family's kitchen table. She loves living in Decatur and frequents the Pub often in search of the latest and greatest offering of India Pale Ale beer.

Mary Jane has used her writing and speaking talents as a public health media specialist, copywriter, entrepreneur, actor, and fundraiser for worthy causes. She proclaimed herself an artist when she turned thirty-five and is grateful to report that she's never been the same. Her three lazy house cats beg to differ, however.

As a former server, Mary Jane touched many lives with her smile. As a writer, she illuminates minds and awakens hearts to life's potential by telling stories that reveal the essence of power, freedom, and grace. Her work has been published in the best selling anthology *Audacious Creativity: 30 Ways to Liberate Your Soulful Creative Energy—and How It Can Transform Your Life.*

To find our more about Mary Jane's current projects or inquire about books, speaking engagements, and other matters, or just to say hello, contact her at www.maryjanebrain.com or www.loveatthepub.com.

Author Mary Jane Mahan